MEASUREMENT 5

Walker Maths Essentials: Measurement 5
1st Edition
Charlotte Walker
Victoria Walker

Designer: Cheryl Smith, Macarn Design
Production controller: Katie McCappin

Acknowledgements
Cover photo courtesy of Shutterstock.

We wish to thank the Boards of Trustees of Darfield and Riccarton High Schools for allowing us to use materials and ideas developed while teaching. Our thanks also go to all past and present colleagues, especially Kath Wilson, who have generously shared their experience and ideas.

For product information and technology assistance,
in Australia call **1300 790 853**;
in New Zealand call **0800 449 725**

For permission to use material from this text or product, please email **aust.permissions@cengage.com**

National Library of New Zealand Cataloguing-in-Publication Data
A catalogue record for this book is available from the National Library of New Zealand.
978 0 17 045045 4

Cengage Learning Australia
Level 7, 80 Dorcas Street
South Melbourne, Victoria Australia 3205

Cengage Learning New Zealand
Unit 4B Rosedale Office Park
331 Rosedale Road, Albany, North Shore 0632, NZ

For learning solutions, visit **cengage.co.nz**

Printed in China by 1010 Printing International Limited.
4 5 6 7 25

Throughout this book:
1 Assume that diagrams are not drawn to scale.
2 Where appropriate, round your answers to a maximum of 2 dp.

CONTENTS

Glossary

Make your own glossary of key terms:

Term	Definition	Picture/Example
Units		
Perimeter		
Area		
Volume		
Capacity		
Polygon		
Compound shape		
Regular shape		
Dimensions		
Vertical		

ISBN: 9780170450454

Cube		
Cuboid		
Face		
Two-dimensional (2D)		
Three-dimensional (3D)		
Prism		
Weight vs Mass		
Kilo		
Centi		
Milli		

The language of measurement

Volume and capacity

- **Volume** measures how much **space** is taken up by an object.
  Units: mm^3, cm^3, m^3.
- **Capacity** measures the **amount that an object can hold**.
  Units: mL, L.
- Sometimes these terms are used interchangeably.

Example: Consider a thermos flask.
Its volume is the amount of space taken up by the flask.
Its capacity is the amount of water that the flask can hold.

Match these words to measurement ideas below.

distance	gradient	load	slope	hot	reach
warm	slant	stretch	heat	steep	pitch
heavy	decline	long	space	wide	fever
incline	far	era	long	age	room
bulk	cold	light	period	icy	flat

Length ____________________

____

____

Angle ____________________

____

____

Time ____________________

____

____

Temperature ____________________

____

____

Volume/Capacity ____________________

____

____

Mass ____________________

____

____

ISBN: 9780170450454

Measuring devices

Match these measuring devices to what they would be used to measure.

tape measure	protractor	scales	tablespoon	thermometer
stopwatch	ruler	compass	measuring cylinder	clinometer
cup	syringe	clock	pedometer	pipette
timer	teaspoon	measuring cup	odometer	spring balance

Length ______________________

____

____

Capacity ______________________

____

____

Mass ______________________

____

____

Angle ______________________

____

____

Time ______________________

____

____

Temperature ______________________

____

____

These pictures might help if you are not familiar with some of the devices.

Spring balance

Odometer

km/h
0042659
Odometer

Clinometer

Pen tube
Protractor
View through here
String and weight

Units

Abbreviations (shortened versions) for units

s	cm	m	c	ha	L
kg	cm^3	min	mg	MB	cal
m^2	g	t	mL	m^3	tbsp
mm	tsp	°C	km	kJ	GB

Complete the table by matching the abbreviations to the units, and write what each is used for.

Unit of measurement	Shortened version	Used to measure (length, mass, volume, capacity, time, temperature, area, energy or data)
Second		
Centimetre	cm	length
Megabyte		
Kilometre		
Degree Celsius		
Kilogram		
Litre		
Millilitre		
Millimetre		
Tablespoon		
Calorie		
Hectare		
Tonne		
Metre		
Minute		
Milligram		
Cup		
Gigabyte		
Teaspoon		
Gram		
Kilojoule		
Cubic metre		
Square metre		
Cubic centimetre		

 ISBN: 9780170450454

Length

- The basic unit for measuring length is the **metre**.
- All other units of length in the metric system are based on the metre.

Use the following chart to help you convert lengths.

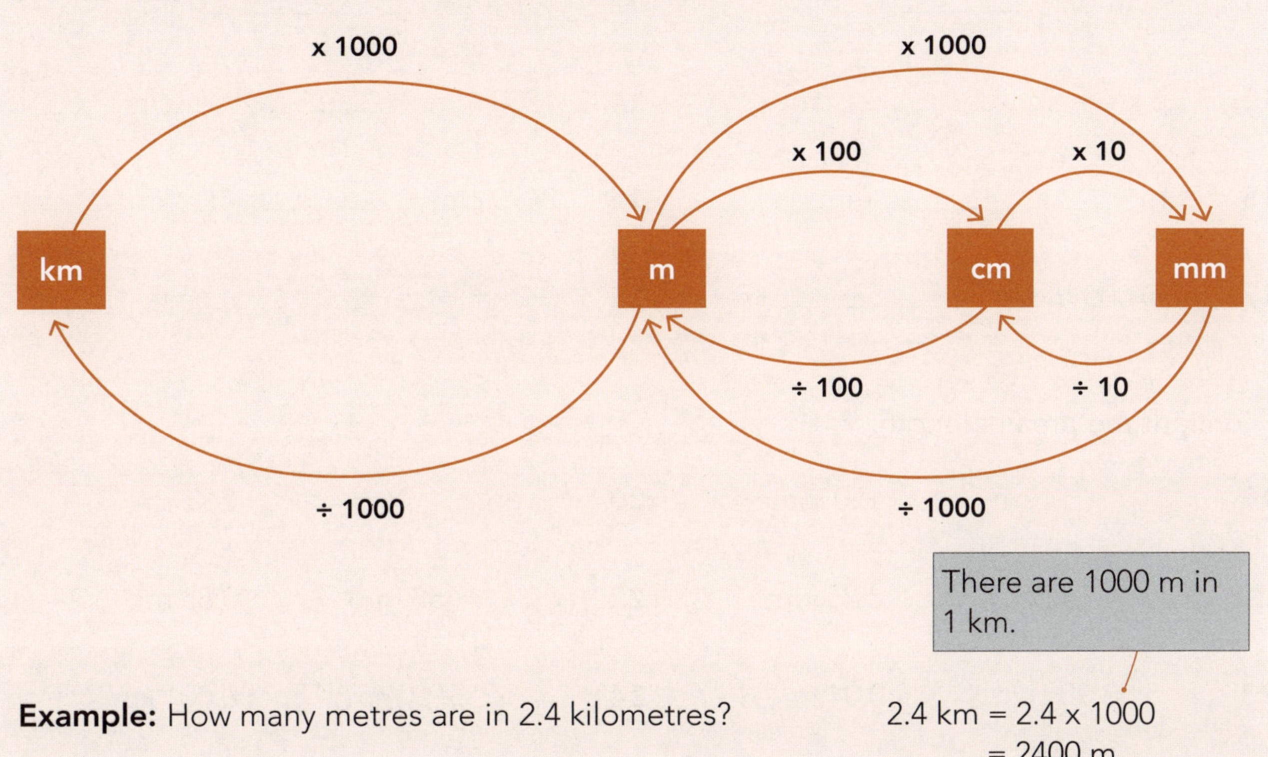

There are 1000 m in 1 km.

Example: How many metres are in 2.4 kilometres?

2.4 km = 2.4 x 1000
= 2400 m

Highlight the correct conversion for each of the following.

1	18 cm	0.0018 m	1.8 mm
		0.018 m	180 mm
2	250 m	2500 cm	250 000 cm
		25 000 cm	25 000 mm
3	3.6 km	3600 cm	360 000 cm
		36 000 cm	360 000 mm
4	543 mm	54.3 m	5.43 cm
		0.543 m	5.43 m
5	2.01 m	2010 cm	20 100 mm
		0.0201 km	2010 mm
6	1.999 km	19 990 cm	199 900 cm
		19 990 m	199.9 m

ISBN: 9780170450454

Convert the following.

7 7 mm = ______________ cm

8 5000 m = ______________ km

9 12 m = ______________ cm

10 4 km = ______________ m

11 19 cm = ______________ m

12 7.5 cm = ______________ mm

13 1.6 km = ______________ cm

14 1200 mm = ______________ m

15 1 m = ______________ mm

16 2690 cm = ______________ km

17 870 000 mm = ______________ km

18 0.2 km = ______________ mm

Highlight the greater length.

19 14 cm 150 mm

20 26 m 265 cm

21 3320 m 3.23 km

22 658 mm 0.65 m

23 3.909 cm 0.04 m

24 9999 mm 0.001 km

Put these lengths in order from shortest to longest. Hint: Rewrite them using the same units.

25

12 cm	1.5 m	21 mm	0.5 km	106 cm

Shortest Longest

26

998 m	989 001 mm	0.989 km	990 m	98 901 cm

Shortest Longest

ISBN: 9780170450454

Circle or highlight the most likely unit of measurement for these items.

27 The length of the classroom.

km m cm mm

28 The thickness of this book.

km m cm mm

29 The length of a pen.

km m cm mm

30 The distance from Auckland to Dunedin.

km m cm mm

31 The width of the whiteboard.

km m cm mm

32 The thickness of glass.

km m cm mm

33 The length of your foot.

km m cm mm

34 The thickness of a cellphone.

km m cm mm

35 The distance you travel to get home.

km m cm mm

36 The length of a car.

km m cm mm

37 The width of your desk.

km m cm mm

38 The distance from earth to the moon.

km m cm mm

Estimating length

From the list on the right, select the most likely for the following.

39 The length of your calculator: ____________

40 The height of a Lego person: ____________

41 The length of a tennis court: ____________

42 The width of a carpark: ____________

43 The distance for a marathon: ____________

44 The width of a door frame: ____________

45 The length of a bank card: ____________

46 The width of a front tooth: ____________

0.81 m
15.5 cm
84 mm
42.2 km
8 mm
40 mm
23.77 m
2.4 m

Mass

- The basic unit for measuring mass is the **gram**.
- All other units of mass in the metric system are based on the gram.
- Mass is often mistakenly called weight.
  Weight is a measure of the pull of gravity on an object and is measured in **newtons**.
  Mass is the amount of matter an object contains and is measured in **grams**.

Use the following chart to help you convert mass.

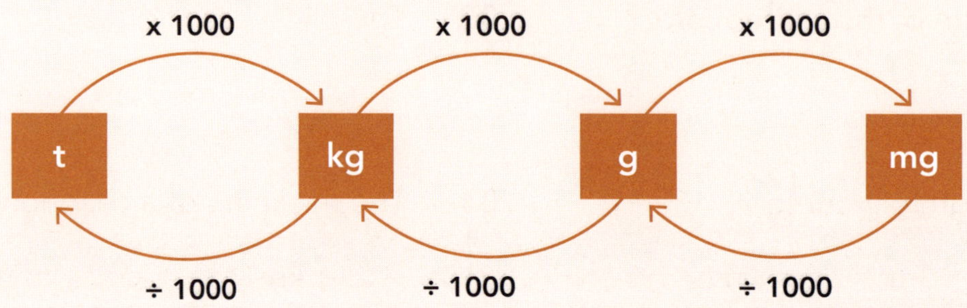

There are 1000 g in 1 kg.

Example: How many grams are in 1.8 kilograms?

1.8 kg = 1.8 x 1000
= 1800 g

Highlight the correct conversion for each of the following.

1	1300 g	0.13 kg	0.013 kg
		1.3 kg	0.013 t
3	0.64 kg	64 000 mg	0.0064 t
		640 g	0.064 t
5	6.76 g	67 600 mg	6760 mg
		676 mg	0.0676 kg
7	0.0099 t	99 000 g	9.99 kg
		9900 g	990 000 mg

2	2.1 t	21 000 kg	2100 kg
		21 000 g	210 000 mg
4	8900 mg	0.089 kg	8.9 g
		0.089 g	89 g
6	32.2 kg	3220 g	32 200 mg
		0.322 t	32 200 g
8	8 870 000 mg	0.00887 t	88 700 g
		887 g	88.7 kg

ISBN: 9780170450454

Convert the following.

9 16 kg = ______________ g

10 0.9 t = ______________ kg

11 630 mg = ______________ g

12 785 g = ______________ kg

13 94 g = ______________ mg

14 236 kg = ______________ t

15 1.4 kg = ______________ mg

16 256 000 g = ______________ t

17 1.3 t = ______________ g

18 7632 mg = ______________ kg

19 341 000 mg = ______________ t

20 0.064 t = ______________ mg

Highlight the greater mass.

21 82 g 80 000 mg

22 43 kg 0.04 t

23 0.11 kg 101 g

24 7545 mg 0.0075 kg

25 0.00969 t 9960 g

26 989 899 mg 0.0009899 t

Put these masses in order from smallest to largest. Hint: Rewrite them using the same units.

27

61 kg	61 100 g	610 000 mg	0.060 t	6100 g

Smallest Largest

28

2.21 t	2021 kg	2201 kg	2.12 t	2 012 000 g

Smallest Largest

ISBN: 9780170450454

Circle or highlight the most likely unit of measurement for these items.

29 The mass of a dog.

t kg g mg

30 The amount of rubbish in a skip.

t kg g mg

31 The mass of an apple.

t kg g mg

32 The mass of a blowfly.

t kg g mg

33 The mass of a truck.

t kg g mg

34 The amount of butter in a cake recipe.

t kg g mg

35 The mass of a sheet of paper.

t kg g mg

36 The mass of your pen.

t kg g mg

37 The mass of a brick.

t kg g mg

38 The mass of this book.

t kg g mg

39 The mass of a chair.

t kg g mg

40 The mass of a whale.

t kg g mg

Estimating mass

From the list on the right, select the most likely masses for the following.

41 The mass of a pen: __________

42 The mass of a piano: __________

43 The mass of a cat: __________

44 The mass of an orange: __________

45 The mass of a train: __________

46 The mass of a pillow: __________

47 The mass of a feather: __________

48 The mass of one litre of water: __________

5000 t
1 kg
0.0082 g
12 g
181.4 kg
4.7 kg
700 kg
250 g

ISBN: 9780170450454

Capacity

- The basic unit for measuring capacity is the **litre**.
- All other units of capacity in the metric system are based on the litre.

Use the following chart to help you convert capacity.

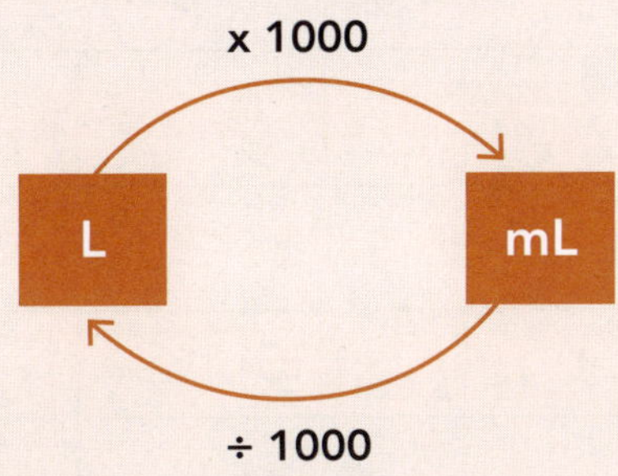

There are 1000 mL in 1 L.

Example: How many millilitres are in 4.2 litres?

4.2 L = 4.2 x 1000
= 4200 mL

Highlight the correct conversion for each of the following.

1	230 mL	0.0023 L	0.023 L
		0.23 L	2.3 L
3	0.0089 L	8.9 mL	0.89 mL
		890 mL	89 mL

2	0.65 L	6500 mL	650 mL
		65 mL	6.5 mL
4	9969 mL	99.69 L	0.09969 L
		9.969 L	0.9969 L

Convert the following.

5 68 L = ______________ mL

6 463 mL = ______________ L

7 6300 mL = ______________ L

8 1 L = ______________ mL

9 24 L = ______________ mL

10 10 500 mL = ______________ L

11 1 mL = ______________ L

12 0.99 L = ______________ mL

ISBN: 9780170450454

Put these capacities in order from smallest to largest. Hint: Rewrite them using the same units.

13

0.99 L	991 mL	1 L	999 mL	0.919 L

Smallest Largest

14

1.1 L	1110 mL	1.101 L	1001 mL	1.01 L

Smallest Largest

Estimating capacity

From the list on the right, select the most likely capacities for the following.

15	The capacity of your drink bottle:	____________	25 L
16	The capacity of the ink tube in a ballpoint pen:	____________	5 mL
17	The capacity of a bucket:	____________	1.5 L
18	The capacity of a kitchen sink:	____________	250 L
19	The capacity of a teaspoon:	____________	22 mL
20	The capacity of a bath:	____________	0.35 mL
21	The capacity of a cup:	____________	250 mL
22	The capacity of a test tube:	____________	1000 L
23	The capacity of a spa pool:	____________	10 L

ISBN: 9780170450454

Conversion cross-number

Fill in the white squares in this cross-number with a digit or a decimal point (•). One decimal point has been put in for you.

1	2	■	3	4	5		■	6
■	7		•			■	8	
9		■	10			11	■	
12	■	13		■	14		15	■
16	17		■	■	■	18		19
■	20		21	■	22		■	
23	■	24		25		■	26	
27		■	28					■
	■	29				■	30	

ACROSS

1 7.5 cm to mm
3 3.124 km to m
7 0.08267 kg to g
8 5.7 cm to mm
9 12 000 mL to L
10 903 mm to cm
13 0.000036 kg to mg
14 510 000 cm to km
16 0.41 L to mL
18 709 000 000 g to t
20 0.0086 t to kg
22 13 000 mL to L
24 8 730 000 mg to kg
26 0.29 m to cm
27 0.057 g to mg
28 42 320 000 cm to km
29 1.51 g to kg
30 0.021 L to mL

DOWN

2 5.82 m to cm
3 0.00396 L to mL
4 0.0016 km to cm
5 27 500 kg to t
6 0.472 kg to g
9 1.94 m to cm
11 3730 mL to L
13 30 800 g to kg
15 0.01 m to mm
17 18 000 mg to g
19 990 cm to m
21 0.00645 km to m
22 1.33 L to mL
23 0.00095 km to mm
25 0.000721 t to g
26 0.000222 km to mm

ISBN: 9780170450454

Appropriate units

- Length is measured in mm, cm, m or km.
- Mass is measured in mg, g, kg or t.
- Capacity is measured in mL or L.

Example: The mass of this bag would be measured in which of the following units?

L **kg** **cm** **t**

The most appropriate answer is kg (kilograms).

Circle or highlight the most appropriate unit of measurement for these items.

1 The amount of cheese in a sandwich.

kg mL g cm

2 The mass of a spider.

t L mm mg

3 The length of a mouse.

km kg cm L

4 The amount of milk in a biscuit recipe.

mL m L mg

5 The mass of a rubbish bin.

cm kg t g

6 The amount of toothpaste in a tube.

kg mg L g

7 The amount of shampoo in a bottle.

g m mg mL

8 The width of a road.

km kg L m

9 The length of a newborn baby.

cm g mm km

10 The mass of your lunch.

mL kg g mg

11 The amount of water in a swimming pool.

mL t L kg

12 The mass of a whale.

t kg g L

13 The mass of a chair.

L kg g mg

14 The length of a sprint.

m mL cm g

15 The amount of salt in a heaped teaspoon.

mL L g mg

16 The mass of a book.

mL kg g mg

ISBN: 9780170450454

Estimating quantities

Use the most appropriate quantities from the list on the right to complete the following sentences. You may need to do some research.

1	The height of a giraffe is most likely to be ____________.	30.5 m
2	The length of the Great Wall of China is most likely to be ____________.	62 mm
3	The capacity of an average human stomach is most likely to be ________.	8 mg
4	The mass of a chicken's egg is most likely to be ____________.	3 kg
5	The width of your thumbnail is most likely to be ____________.	5.2 km
6	The height of the Eiffel Tower is most likely to be ____________.	9.5 t
7	The mass of a gorilla is most likely to be ____________.	2500 L
8	The length of a netball court is most likely to be ____________.	1 250 000 L
9	The height of your school desk is most likely to be ____________.	200 g
10	The capacity of an average human bladder is most likely to be ________.	400 mL
11	The mass of a tractor is most likely to be ____________.	760 mm
12	The school cross-country is most likely to be ____________.	160 kg
13	The distance between the pupils in your eyes is most likely to be ____________.	1.2 cm
14	The mass of sugar in a full cup is most likely to be ____________.	21 196 km
15	The capacity of the school swimming pool is most likely to be ________.	1.5 L
16	The volume of air in a car is most likely to be ____________.	290 cm
17	The capacity of a large saucepan is most likely to be ____________.	63 g
18	The height of the ceiling in your classroom is most likely to be ________.	5.4 m
19	The mass of a newborn baby is most likely to be ____________.	324 m
20	The mass of a fly is most likely to be ____________.	8 L

ISBN: 9780170450454

Word questions

1 Two litres of milk is shared equally between eight children. How much milk will each child receive? Write your answer in mL.

____

2 Casey ran 2.56 km and his friend Mason ran 2650 m. Who ran further and by how much?

____

3 A cricket player drinks on average 228 mL at each drink break. How many litres does a player drink during seven drink breaks?

____

4 In a zoo there are seven 'big cats'. They each need 9 kg of meat per day. How many tonnes would they eat per month (30 days)?

____

5 Karen has some ribbon for wrapping presents. Each present needs a length of 35 cm. How many presents can she wrap with 1.2 m of ribbon?

____

6 Ben has picked 32 beans from his garden. They weigh a total of 2.4 kg. On average, how much does bean weigh? Write your answer in grams (g).

____

7 **a** Parking spaces are to be marked out in a new carpark. Each needs to be 240 cm wide. How many spaces could you fit in an area that is 125 m long?

____

b If the paint strip between each park needs to be 10 cm wide, does this change your answer?

____

8 Nancy killed 95 wasps in a nest. If each wasp had a mass of 12 mg, calculate the total mass of the wasps. Write your answer in grams (g).

____

9 A ream of paper (500 sheets) is 5.2 cm thick. Calculate the thickness of one sheet of paper. Write your answer in millimetres (mm).

____

ISBN: 9780170450454

Scales

Reading scales

- Find **zero** on the scale to make sure that you read in the **correct direction**.
- If zero is not on the scale, make sure you read from **smaller values to larger values**.
- Include **units** in your answer.
- **Think** about your answer. Does it seem reasonable?

Example:

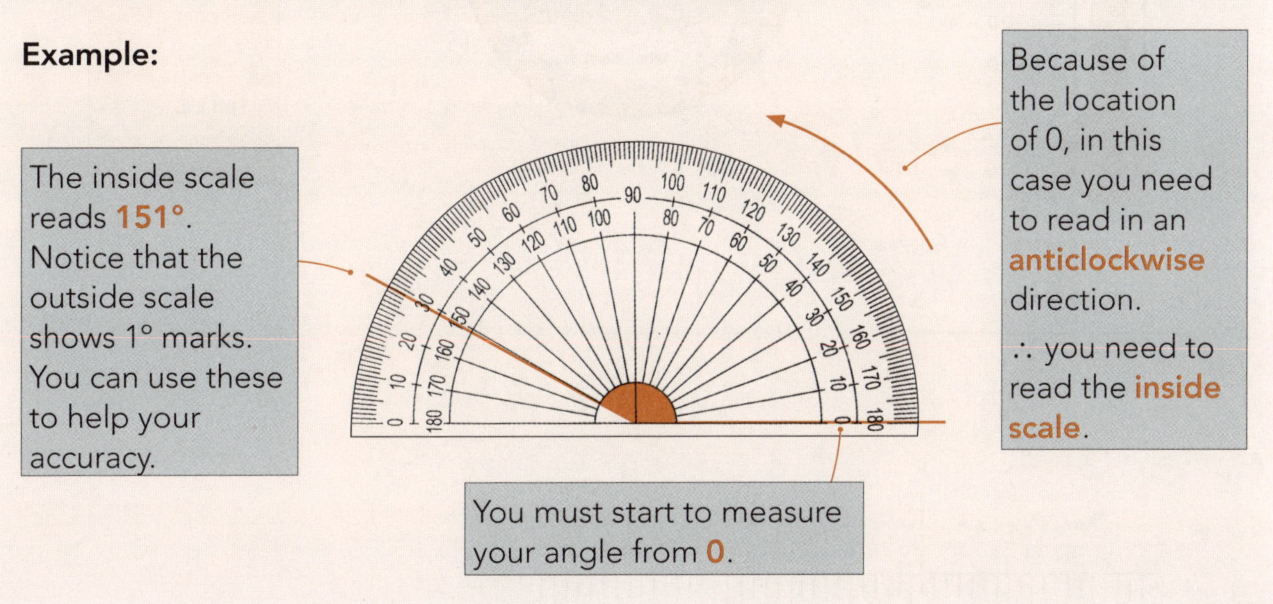

Identify the measurements shown in these diagrams.

1

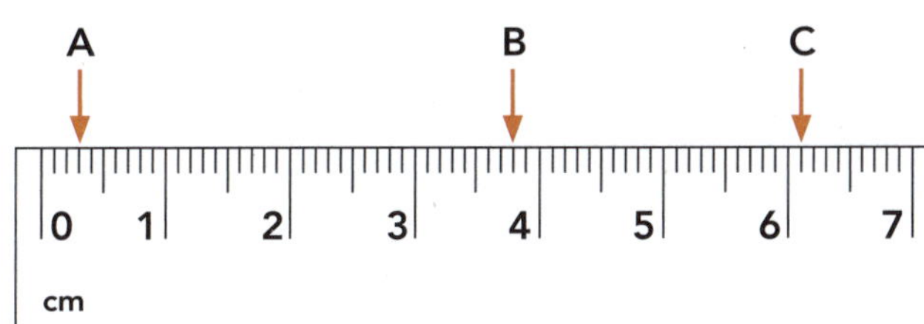

A = ______________________

B = ______________________

C = ______________________

2

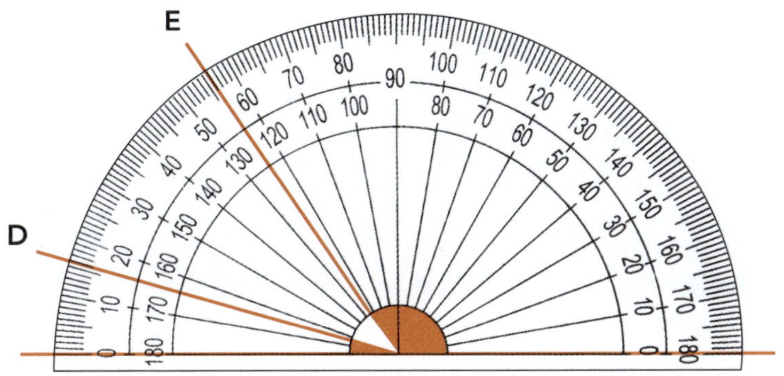

D = ______________________

E = ______________________

3

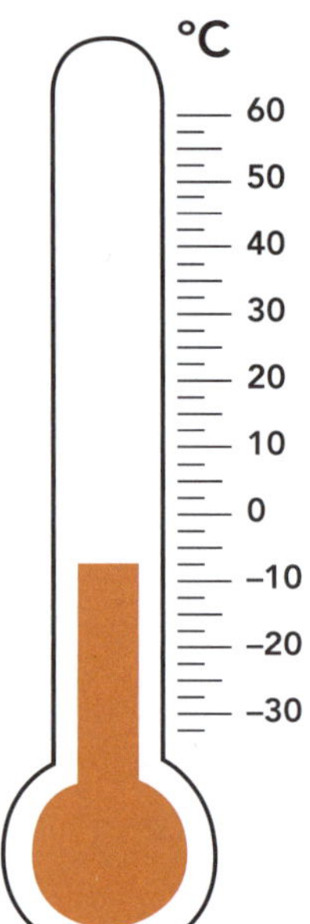

____

4

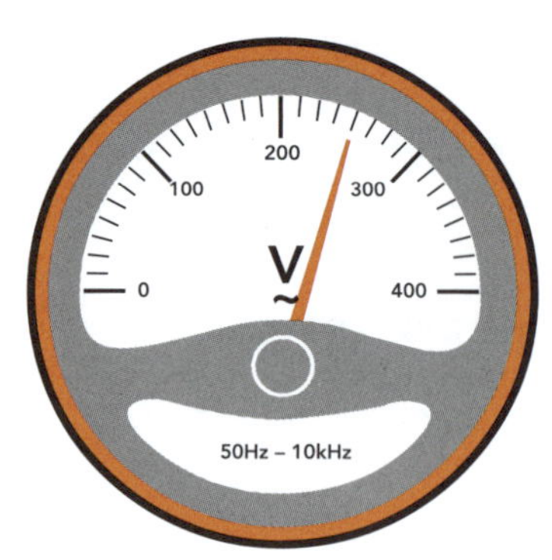

____

5

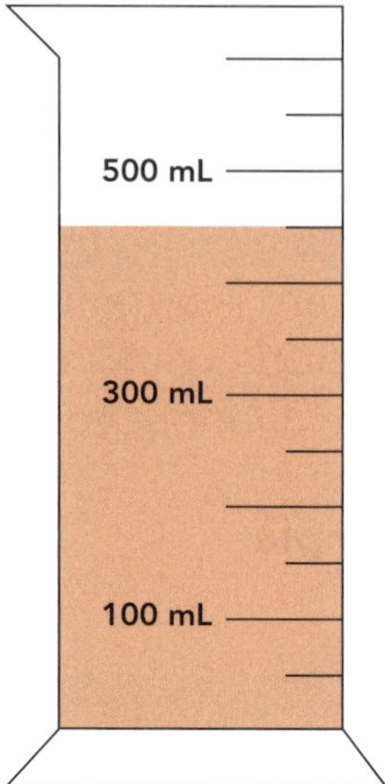

____

6

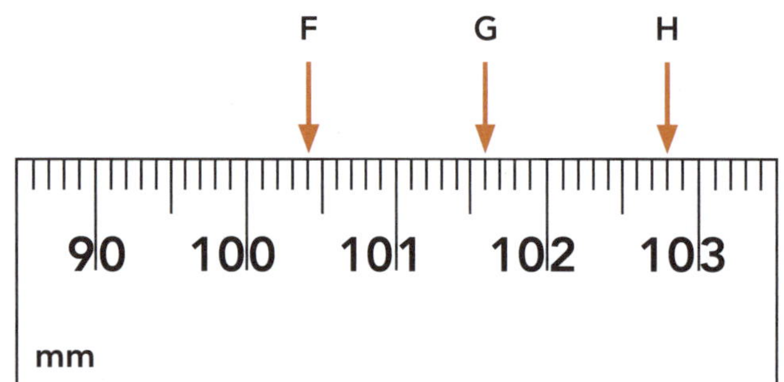

F = ______________________

G = ______________________

H = ______________________

7

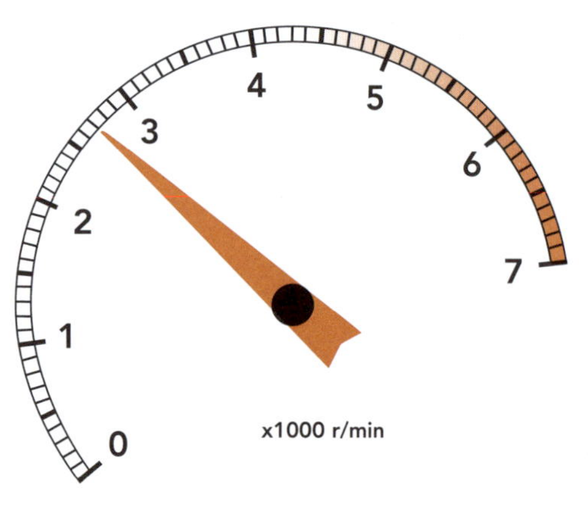

Speed = ______________________

8

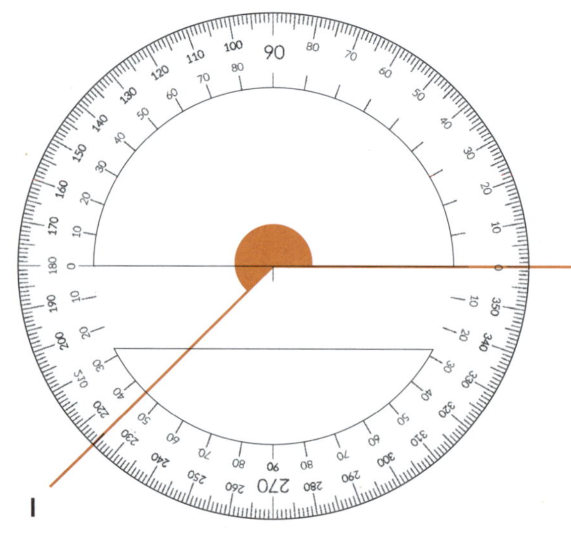

I = ______________________

 ISBN: 9780170450454

Showing values on scales

Colour the diagrams or add an arrow to show these measurements.

1 127°

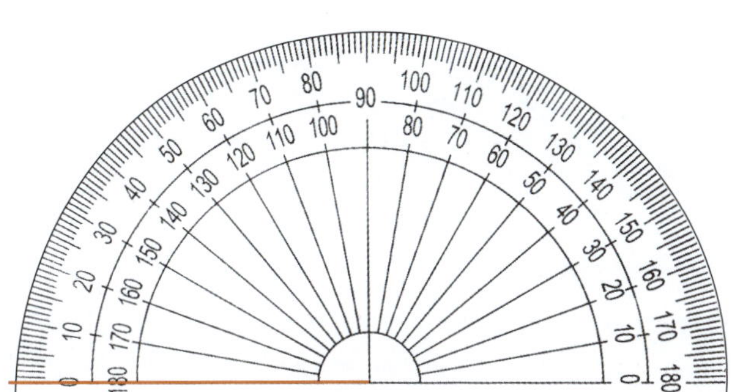

2 95 km/h

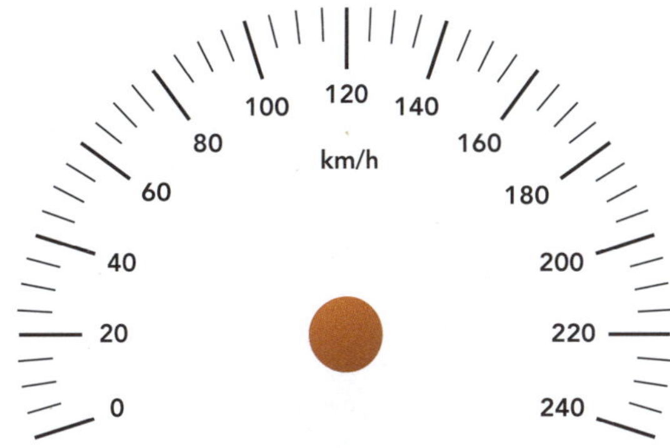

3

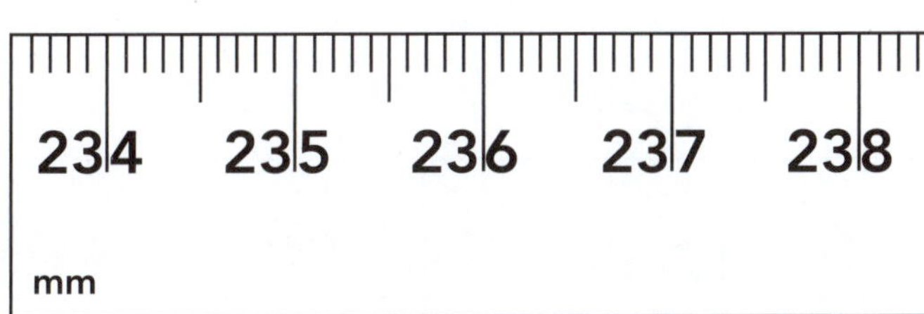

A = 236.7 mm

B = 238.1 mm

C = 235.4 mm

4 38 V

5 170 mL

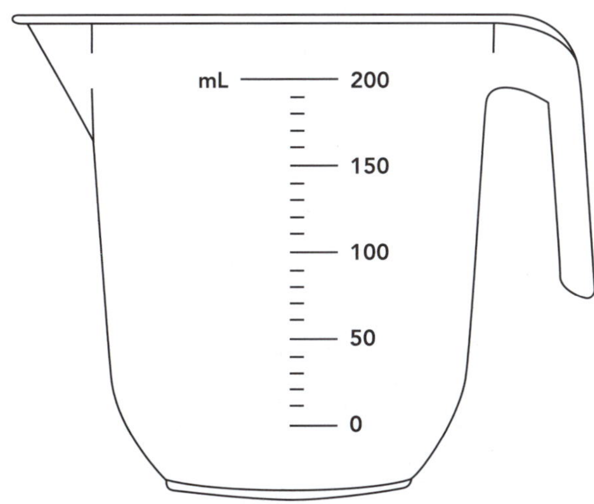

ISBN: 9780170450454

6 335°

7 125 mL

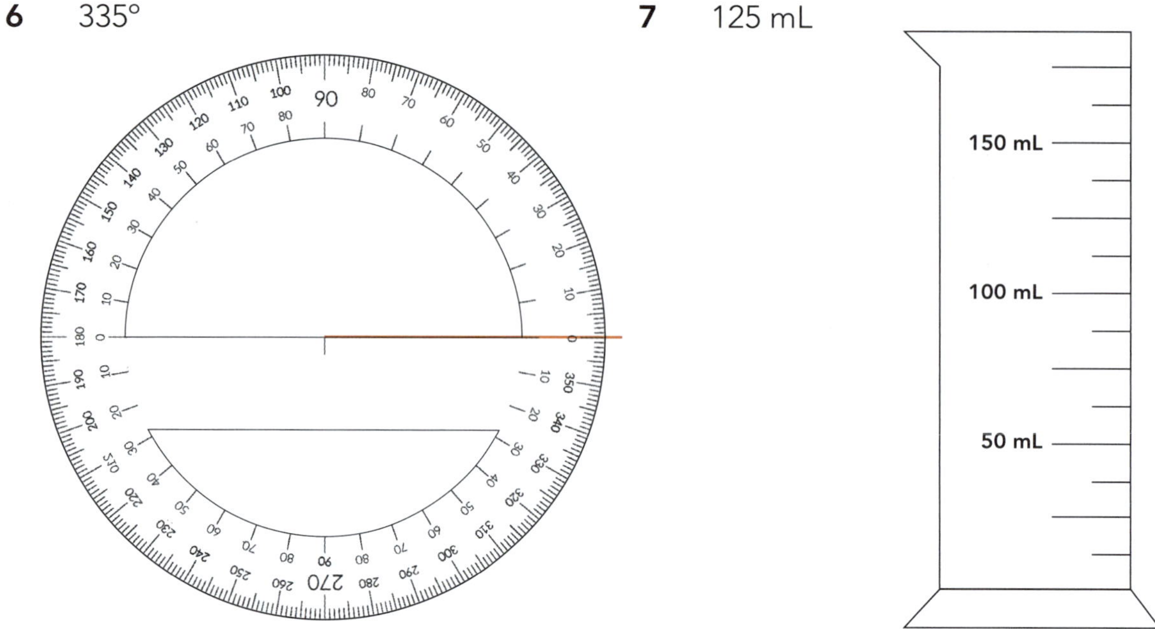

8 Write decimal values for each point along the ruler. Choose the most appropriate values from the list below. You will not need all the values on the list.

0.44	0.49	0.01	0.26	0.39	0.86
0.11	0.83	0.08	0.23	0.74	0.69
0.53	0.17	0.58	0.62	0.65	0.31

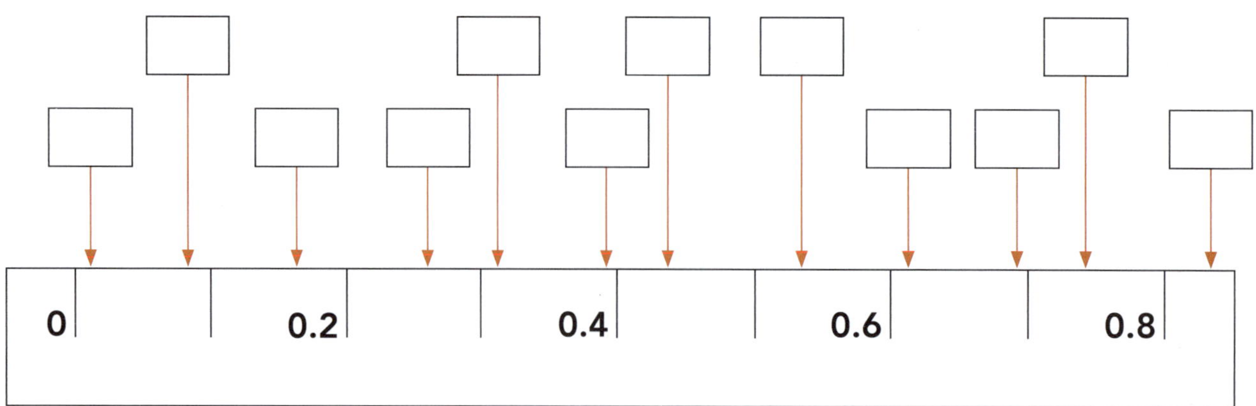

ISBN: 9780170450454

Perimeter

Shapes with linear sides

- The perimeter is the **distance around the outside** of a two-dimensional (2D) shape.
- To find the perimeter, you need to **start at one corner** and **add** the distances around the outside of the shape.
- You can add lengths only if they are in the **same units**, so you may need to do some conversions.
- 'Regular' means all the sides and angles in a figure are the same.

Examples:

1

Opposite sides are the same because this is a rectangle.

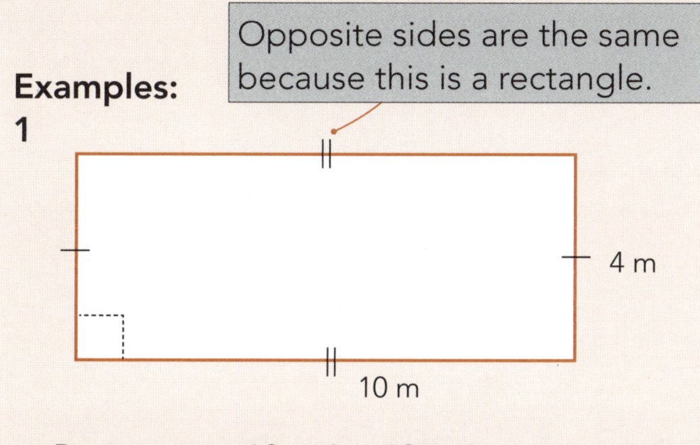

Perimeter = 10 + 4 + 10 + 4
= 28 m

2

These symbols tell you that all the sides are equal.

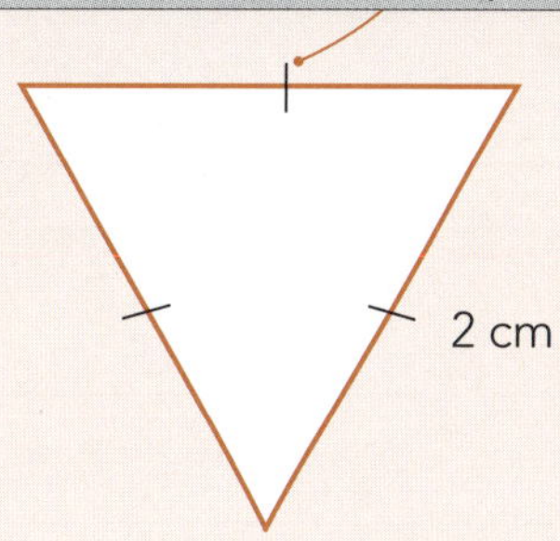

Perimeter = 2 + 2 + 2
= 6 cm

Calculate the perimeters of these shapes.

1

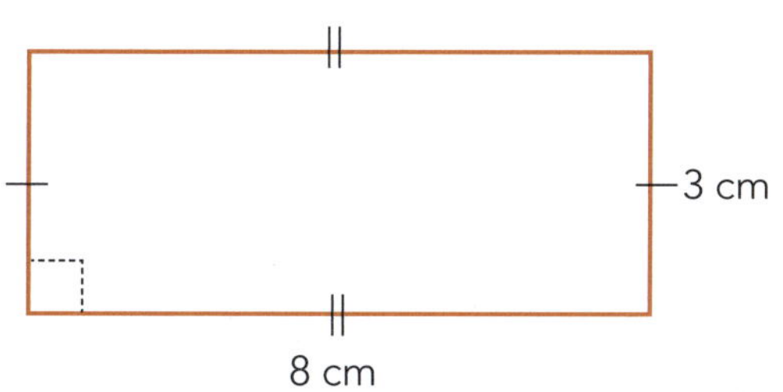

____

____

2

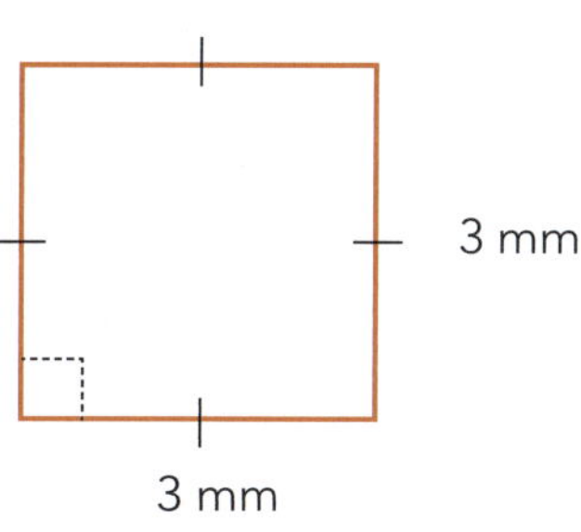

____

____

3

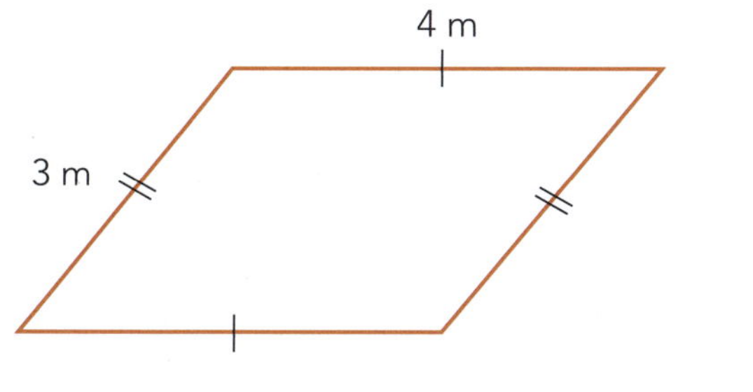

____

____

4

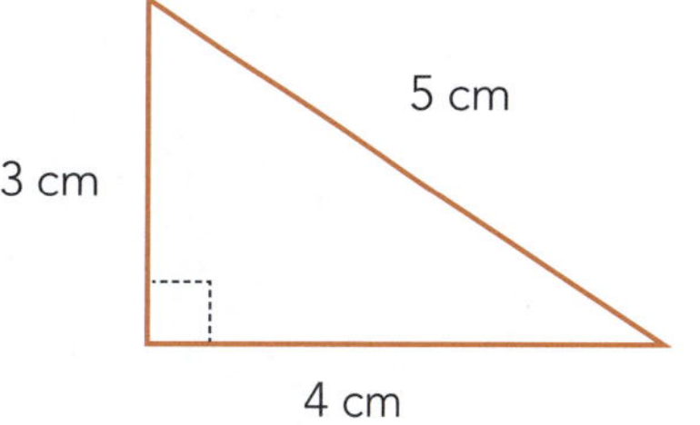

____

____

ISBN: 9780170450454

5

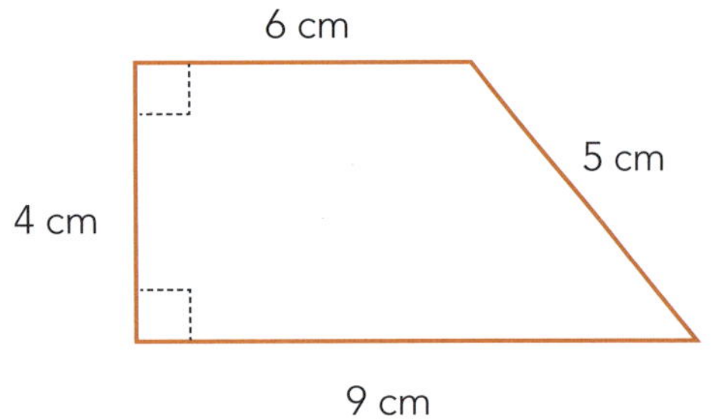

6

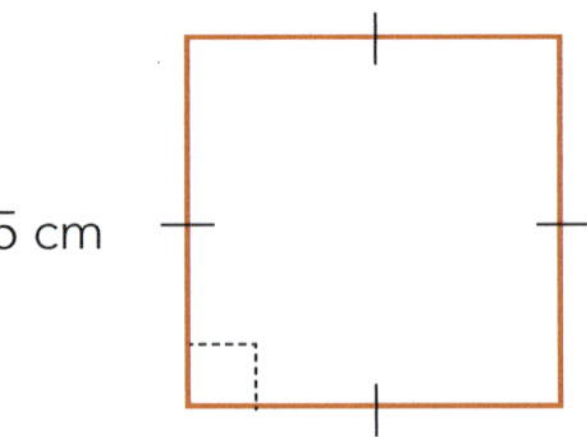

7

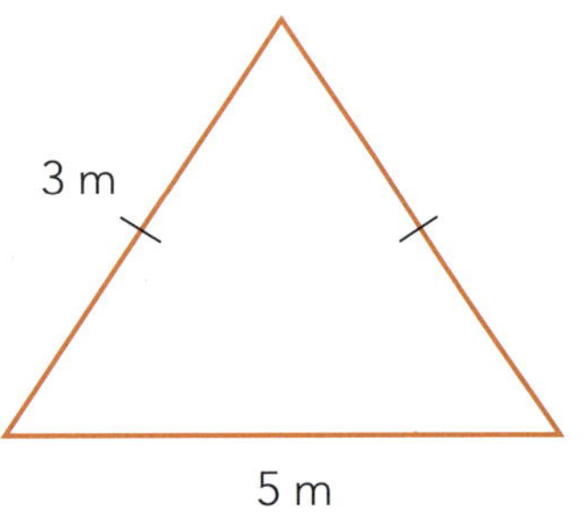

8 This is a regular pentagon.

9

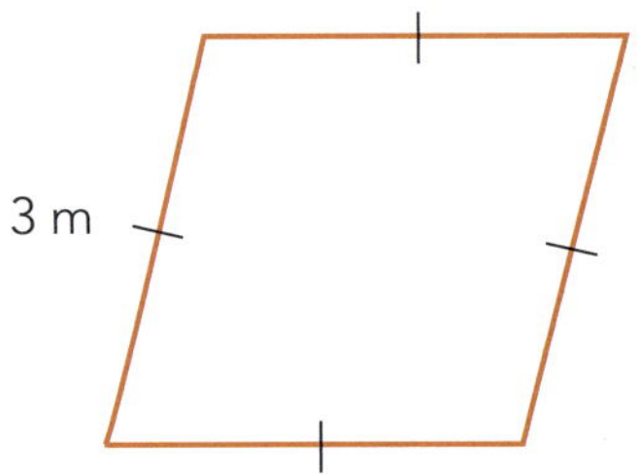

10

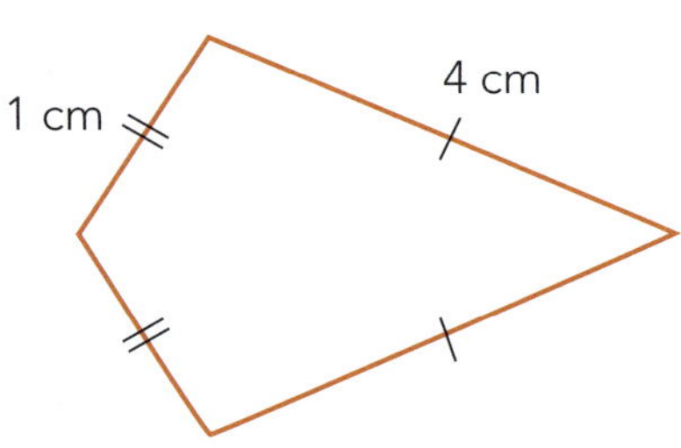

11

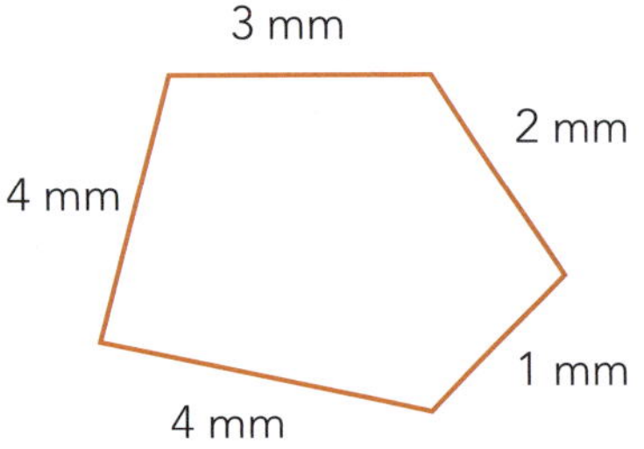

12

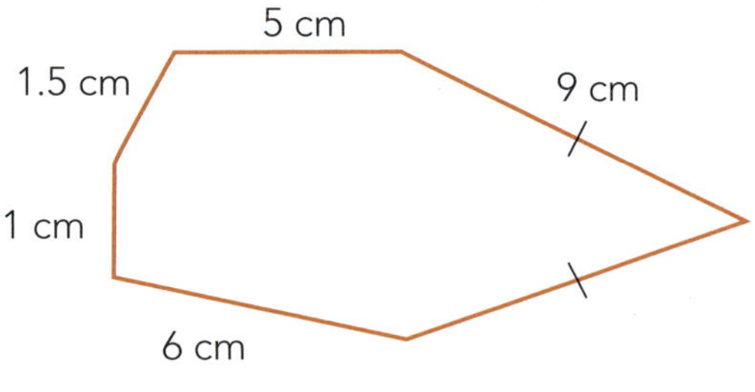

 ISBN: 9780170450454

13

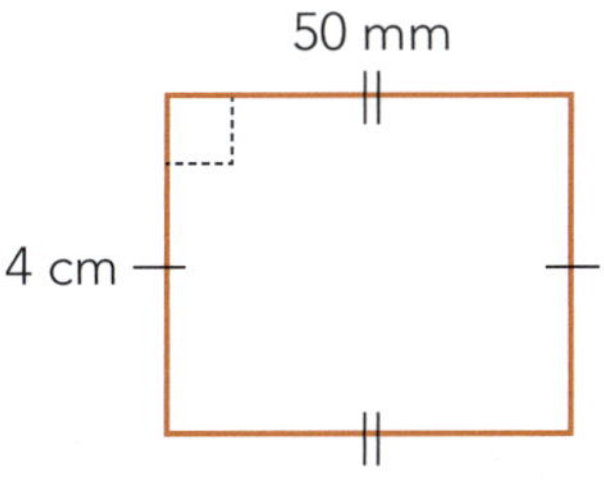

14

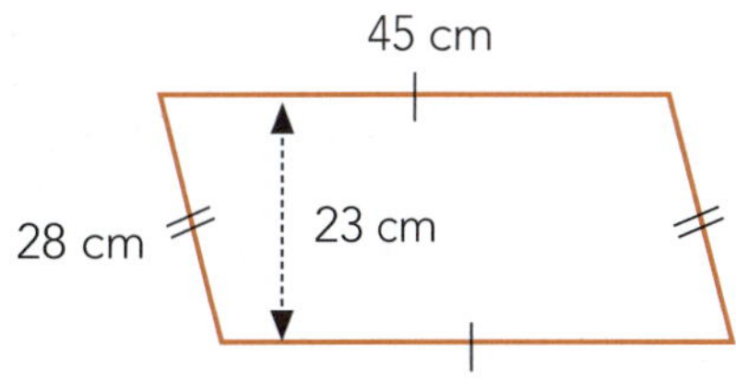

15

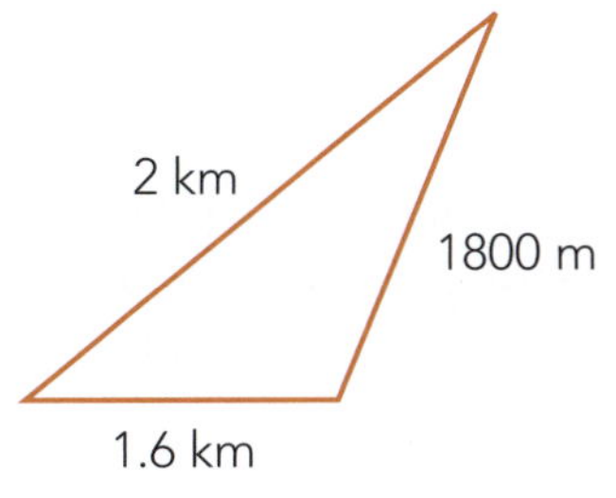

16

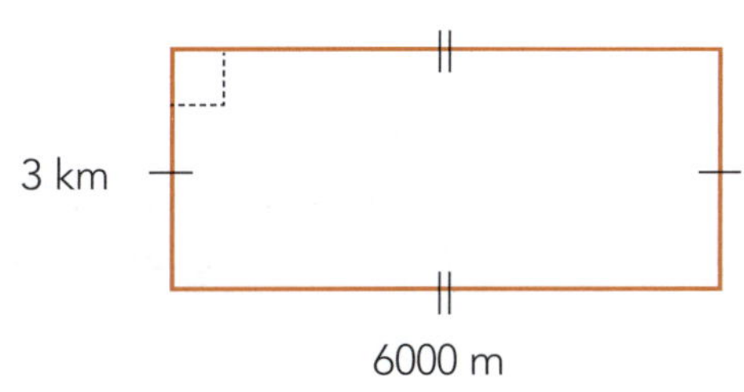

17 Write your answer in metres (m).

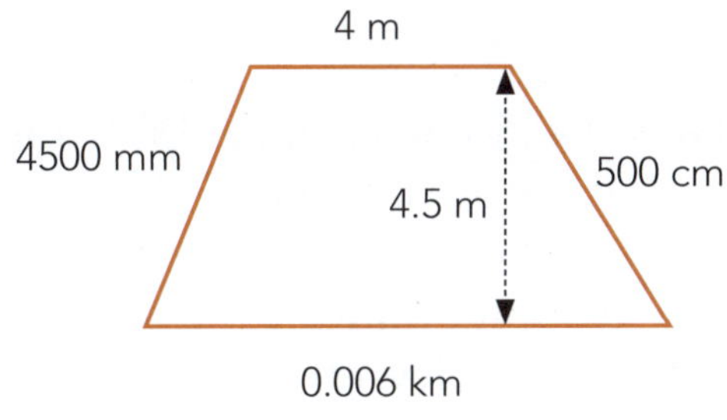

18 Write your answer in centimetres (cm).

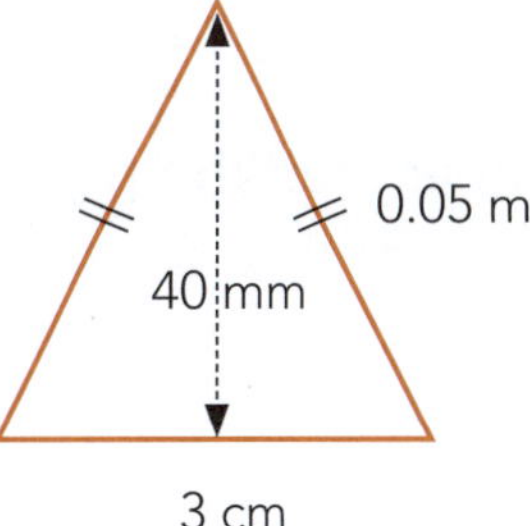

Answer the following questions.

19 The perimeter of this rectangle is 30 m. Calculate the length of side *h*.

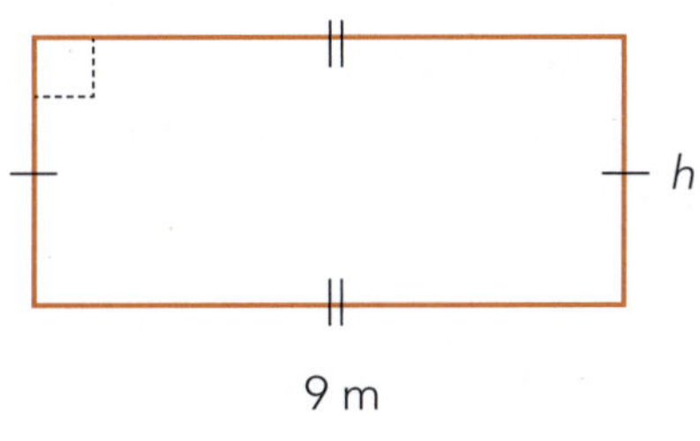

20 The perimeter of this square is 48 cm. Calculate the length of the sides (*s*).

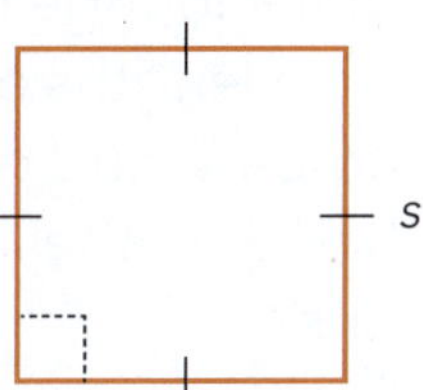

21 The perimeter of this equilateral triangle is 96 km. How long is each side?

22 The perimeter of this regular pentagon is 80 cm. How long is each side?

23 Sally wants to fence her rectanglar property. It is 250 m wide and 225 m long. How much fencing will she need in total?

24 Juanita is laying a rope on the ground to create an area for playing volleyball. The sides need to be 19 m and 8 m. How much rope will she need?

25 Eru measured the perimeter of the window in his bedroom and found it was 14 m. The width was 4 m. How high is the window?

26 Ella is sewing rectangular table mats which measure 0.4 m by 0.25 m. She wants to sew a rectangle of braid 6 cm from the outer edges of each mat. What length of braid will she need for each mat? Write your answer in metres (m).

27 A rectangular lounge has a perimeter of 20 m. The lengths of the sides are whole numbers, and one side is 2 m longer than the other. What are its dimensions?

28 At the start of training, Susie had to jog five times around the outside of a tennis court. If the court measured 23.8 m by 8.2 m, how far did she jog?

ISBN: 9780170450454

Circles

- The perimeter of a circle has a special term: **circumference**.
- π (pi) is about **3.14**, and represents the number of diameters needed to make up the length of the circumference.
- Because π is an irrational number, you will always need to **round your answers** appropriately, and indicate the number of decimal places.

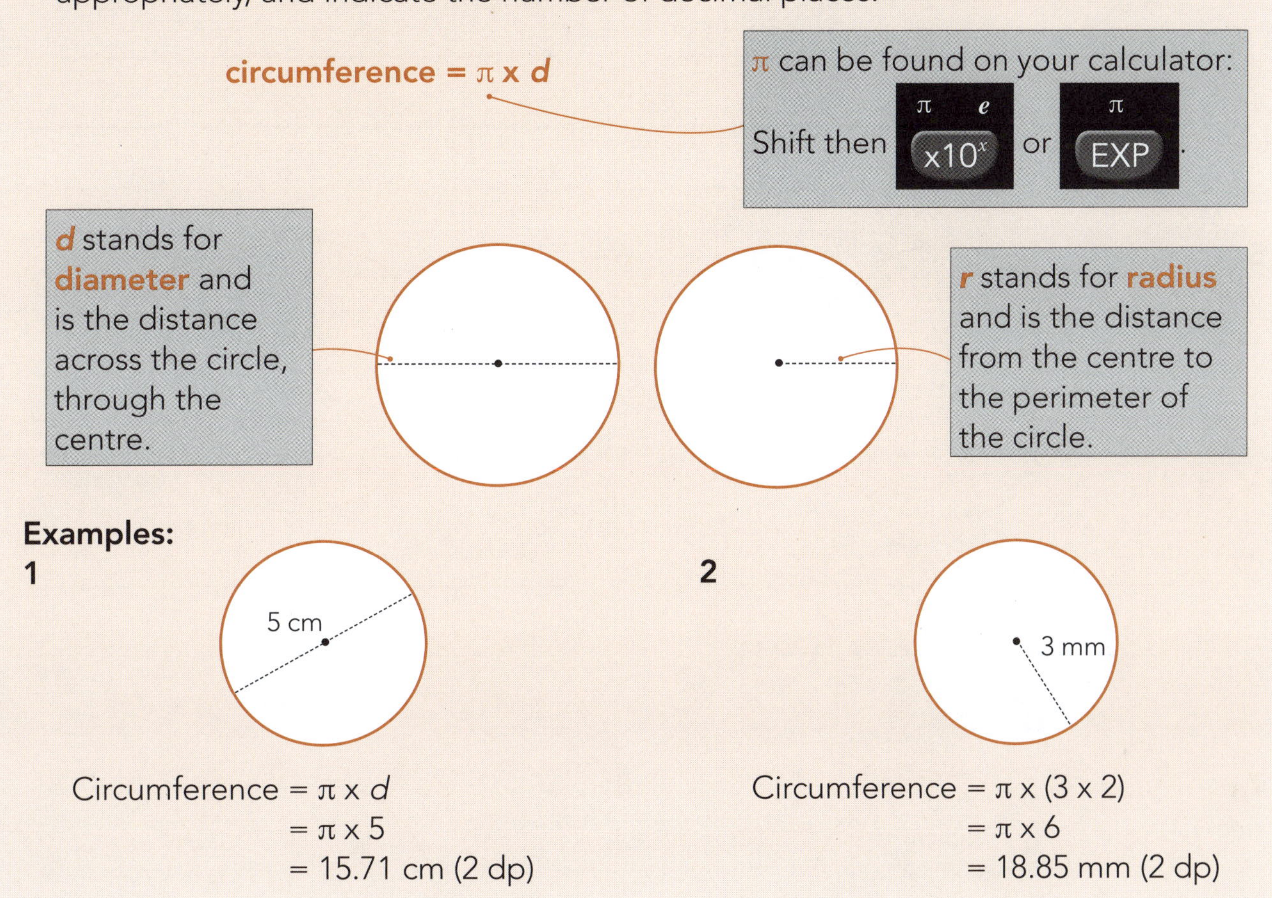

Examples:

1

Circumference = π x *d*
= π x 5
= 15.71 cm (2 dp)

2

Circumference = π x (3 x 2)
= π x 6
= 18.85 mm (2 dp)

Calculate the circumferences of these circles.

1

8 m

____

____

2

2 km

____

____

ISBN: 9780170450454

3

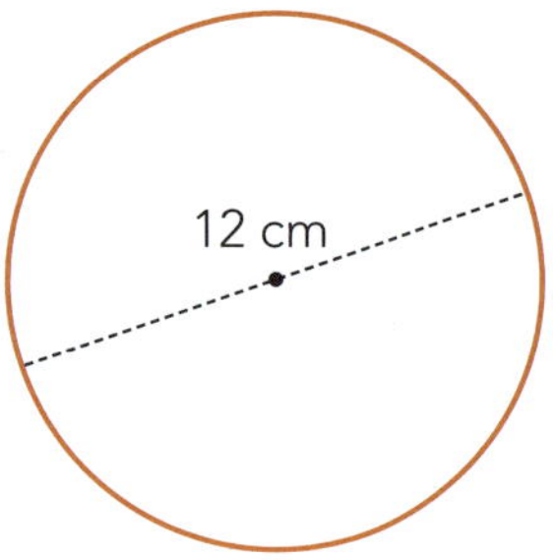

4

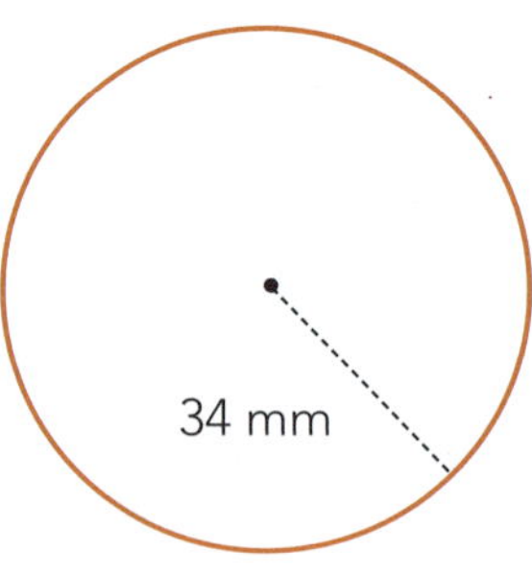

5

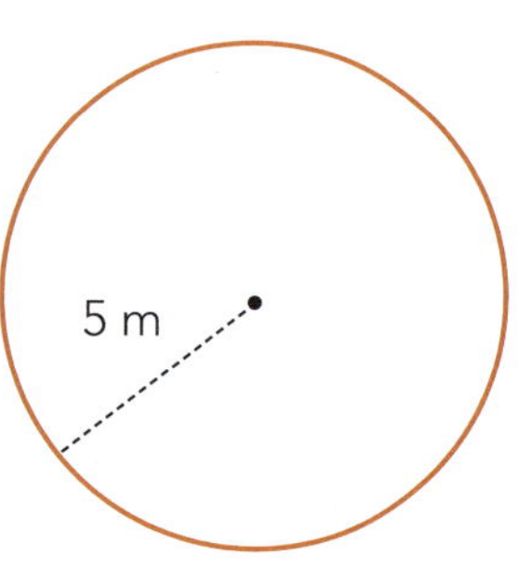

6

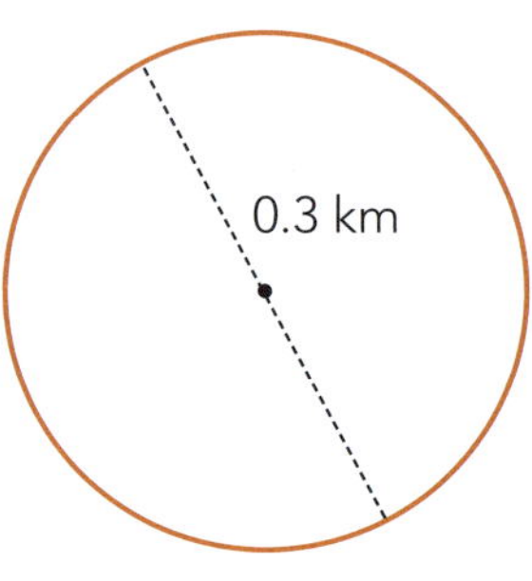

7

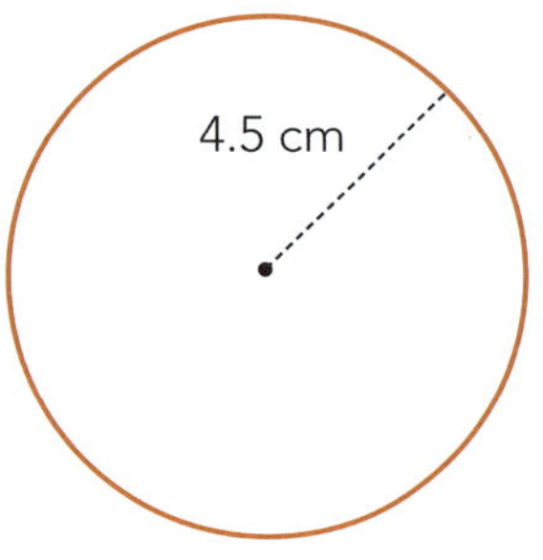

8

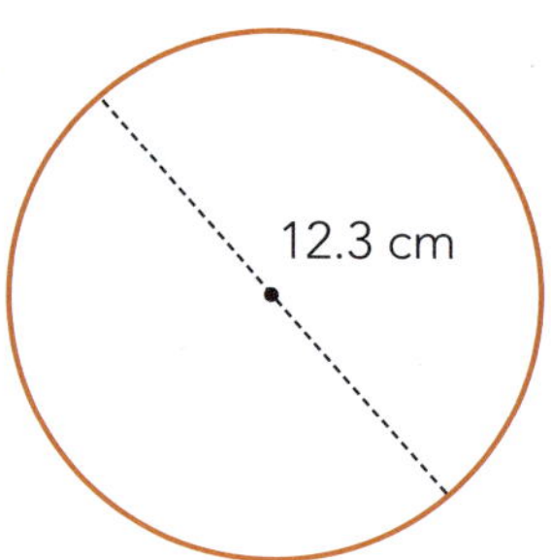

9 A circle with a diameter of 11 m.

10 A circle with a radius of 3 km.

ISBN: 9780170450454

11

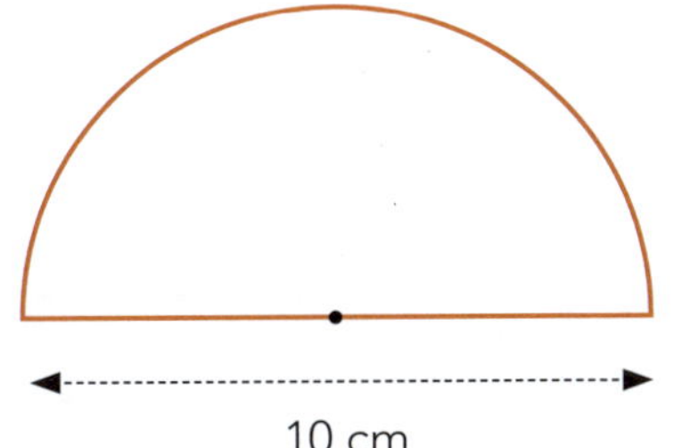

12

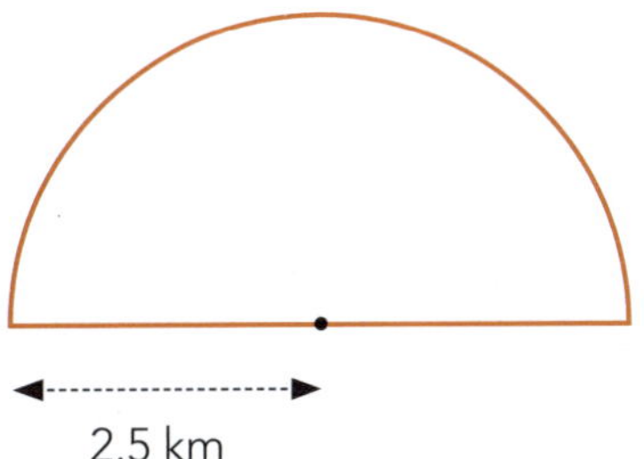

13

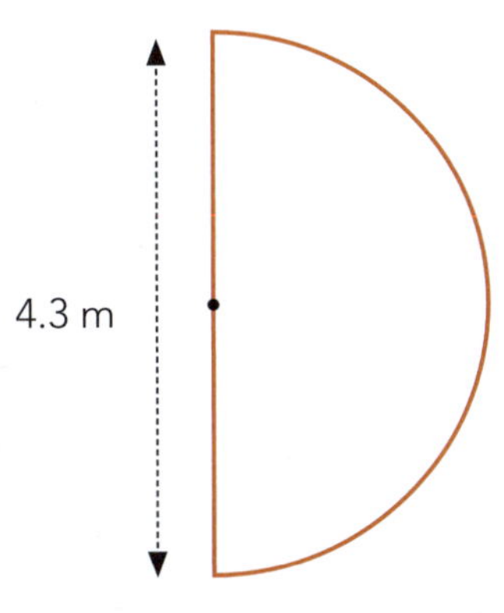

14

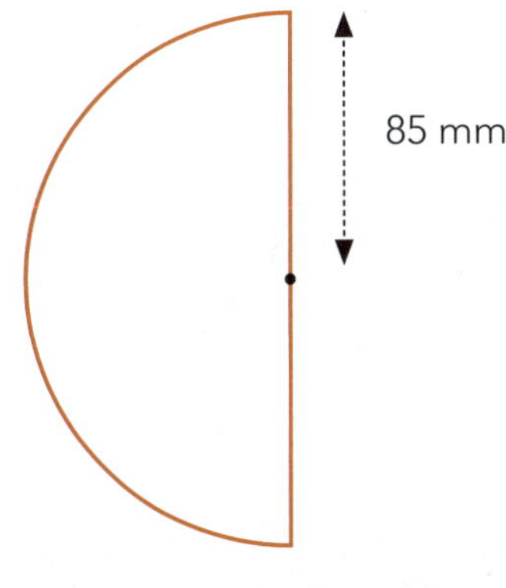

15

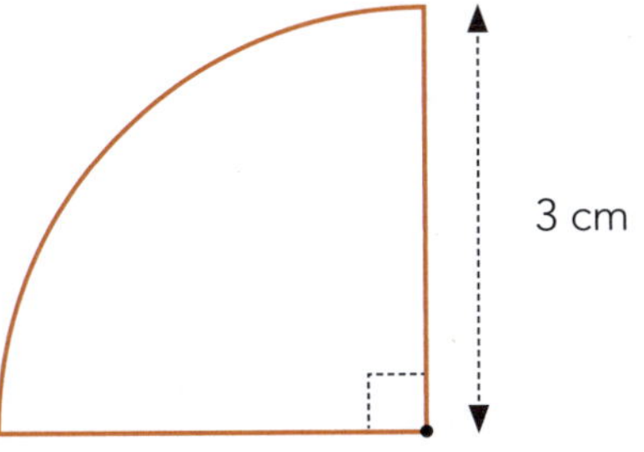

16

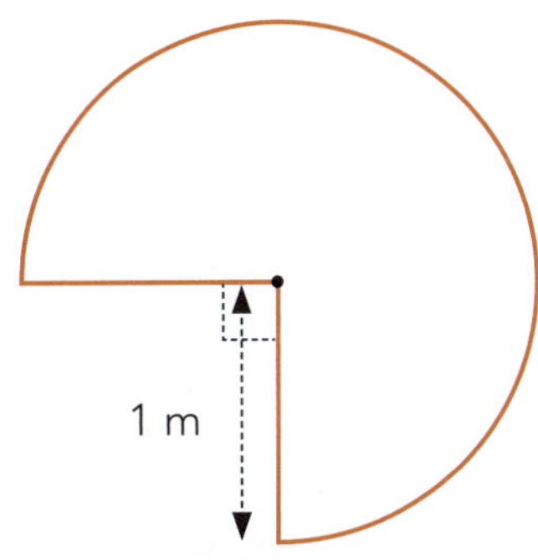

ISBN: 9780170450454

Compound shapes

- A compound shape is one made up of **several 'basic' shapes**.
- Not all measurements may be written on diagrams, so you might need to calculate some.

Examples:

1

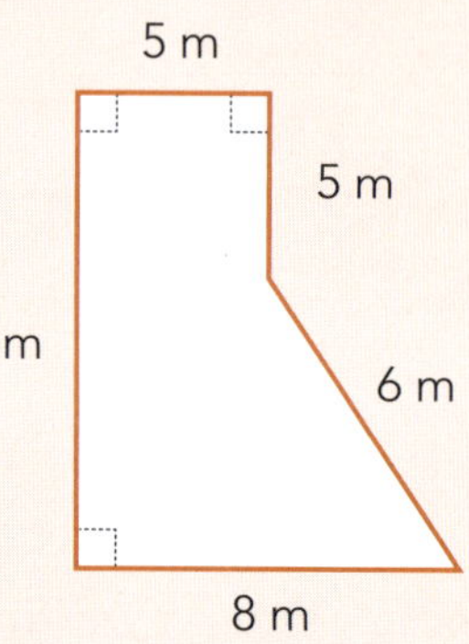

Perimeter = 5 + 5 + 6 + 8 + 9
= 33 m

2

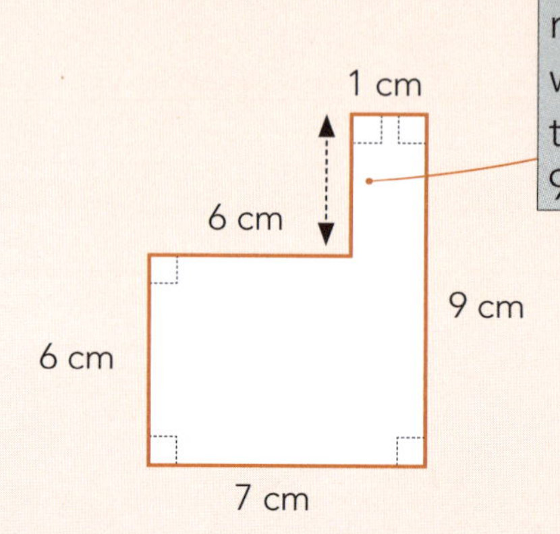

There is a value missing here, which you need to calculate.
9 – 6 = 3 cm

Perimeter = 6 + 6 + 3 + 1 + 9 + 7
= 32 cm

Calculate the perimeters of these compound shapes.

1

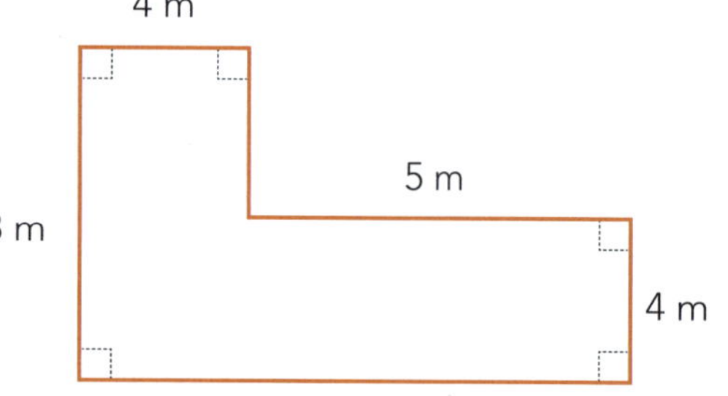

2

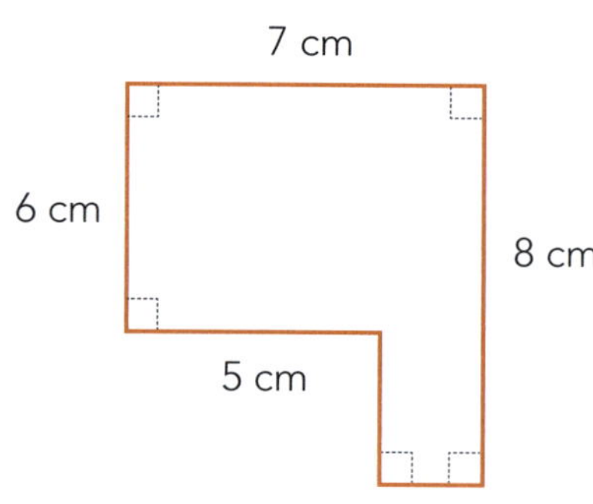

3

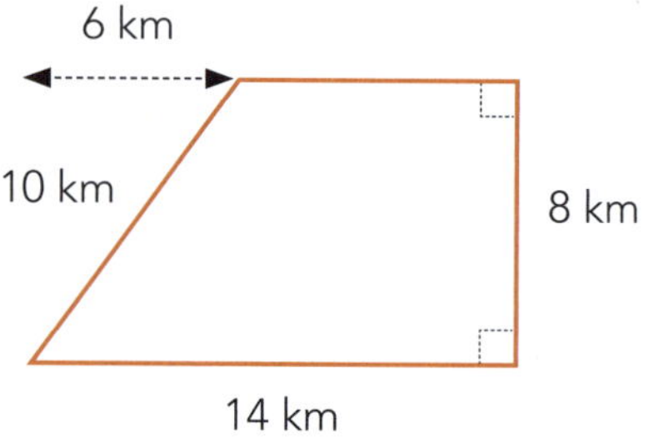

4

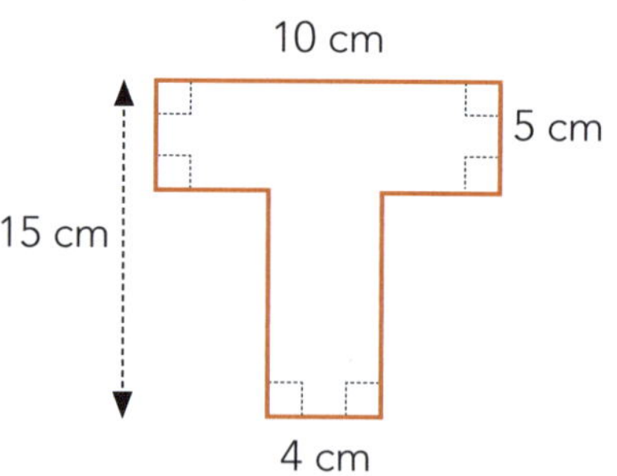

 ISBN: 9780170450454

5

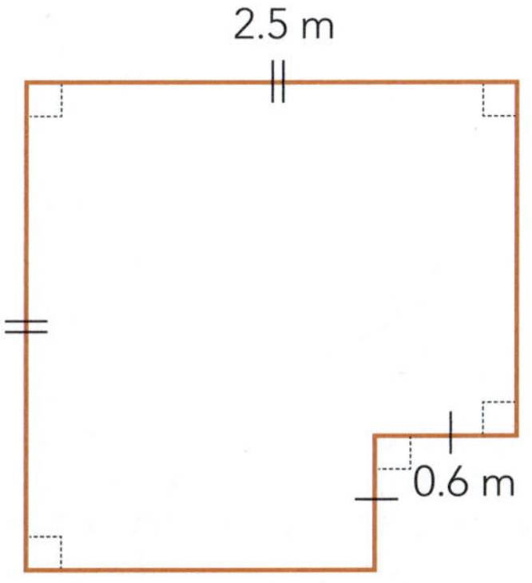

6

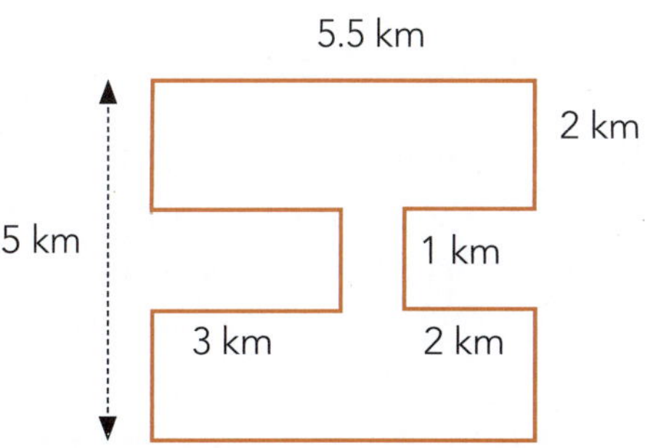

7

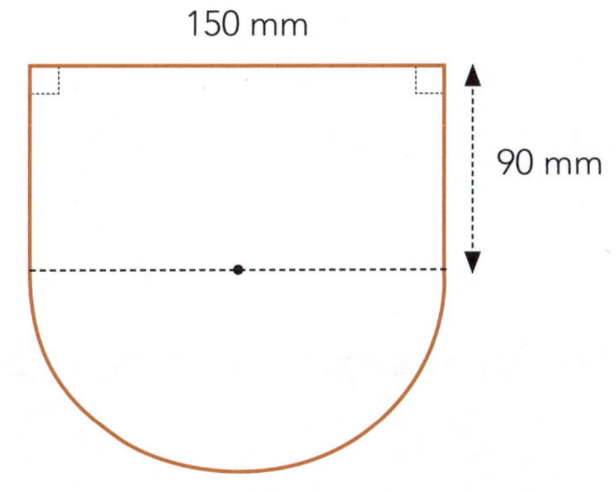

8

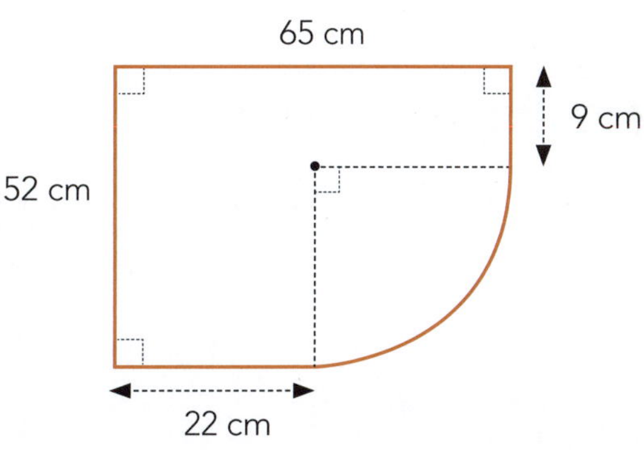

9

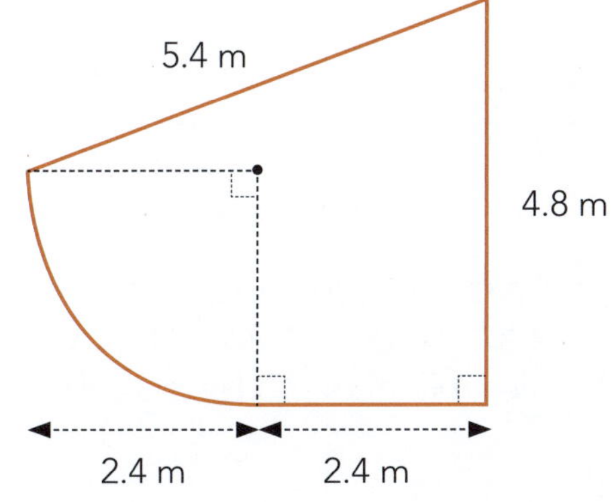

10 Write your answer in centimetres (cm).

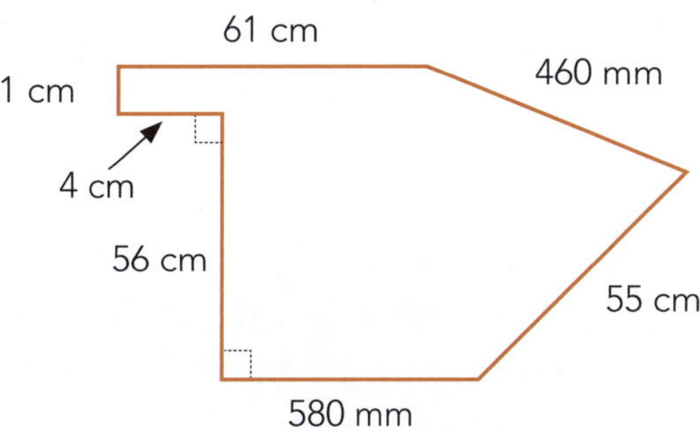

ISBN: 9780170450454

Word questions

Word questions are easier if you follow these steps:

Step 1: Identify the shape.
Step 2: Sketch a diagram.
Step 3: Add the measurements to the diagram.
Step 4: Calculate the perimeter.

Example: In the botanical gardens they are creating a semicircular pond. There will be a circular island in the middle as a refuge for birds. The radius of the pond will be 6.5 m, and the island will have a diameter of 3 m. Calculate the total length of the edging required for the pond and the island.

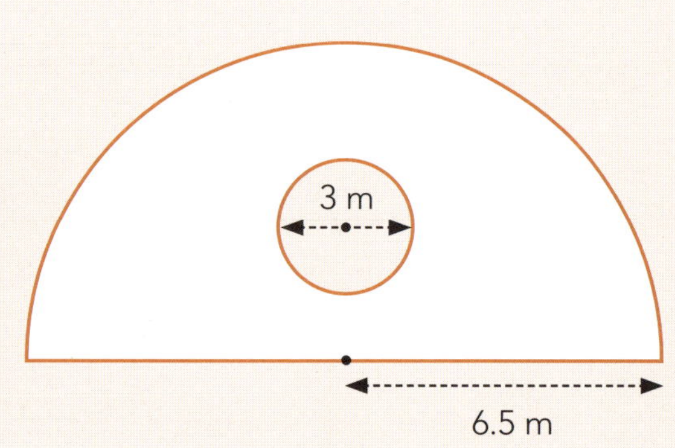

$$\text{Perimeter of pond} = \frac{\pi d}{2} + d$$
$$= \frac{13\pi}{2} + 13$$
$$= 33.42 \text{ m (2 dp)}$$

$$\text{Circumference of the island} = \pi d$$
$$= \pi \times 3$$
$$= 9.42 \text{ m (2 dp)}$$

Total length of edging = 42.84 m (2 dp)

Sketch a diagram for each question before you calculate the answers.

1 **a** Edward has 181.2 m of fencing available for a square paddock. If he uses it all, what will be the length of one side of the paddock?

b How long would each side be if he uses all his fencing but one side of the square is an existing fence?

2 **a** A circular pool has a diameter of 4.3 m. What length of tiling will be needed to go around the edge of the pool?

b If each tile (including the gap between each tile) takes up 7 cm, how many tiles will need to be bought?

ISBN: 9780170450454

3 A square wedding cake has three layers.

- The length of one side of the bottom layer is 30 cm.
- The sides of the next two layers are each 10 cm shorter than that of the layer below.
- One strip of ribbon will go around the sides of each cake, with no overlap of the ends.

a Calculate the total length of ribbon needed.

b Suppose the cake was circular, with the diameter of the bottom layer 30 cm, and the diameters getting 10 cm shorter for each layer. Calculate the total length of ribbon needed.

4 **a** A regular hexagon is cut in half through two of its vertices (corners). The long side of the shape created is twice as long as the short sides. If the short sides are 12 cm long, calculate its perimeter.

b A similar half-hexagon is part of a patchwork quilt. It needs to be as large as possible and have an edging of braid. If there is 95 cm of braid available, what will be the lengths of its short sides?

5 The enclosure for the rabbit hutch is to:

- be rectangular
- be 2.7 m by 1.8 m
- be made from wire netting
- have a post at each corner and posts spaced every 90 cm along the sides
- have a wooden gate that is 90 cm wide and located between two of the posts.

a What length of wire netting will be needed?

b How many posts will need to be bought?

ISBN: 9780170450454

Challenge 1

Calculate the perimeter of this shape.

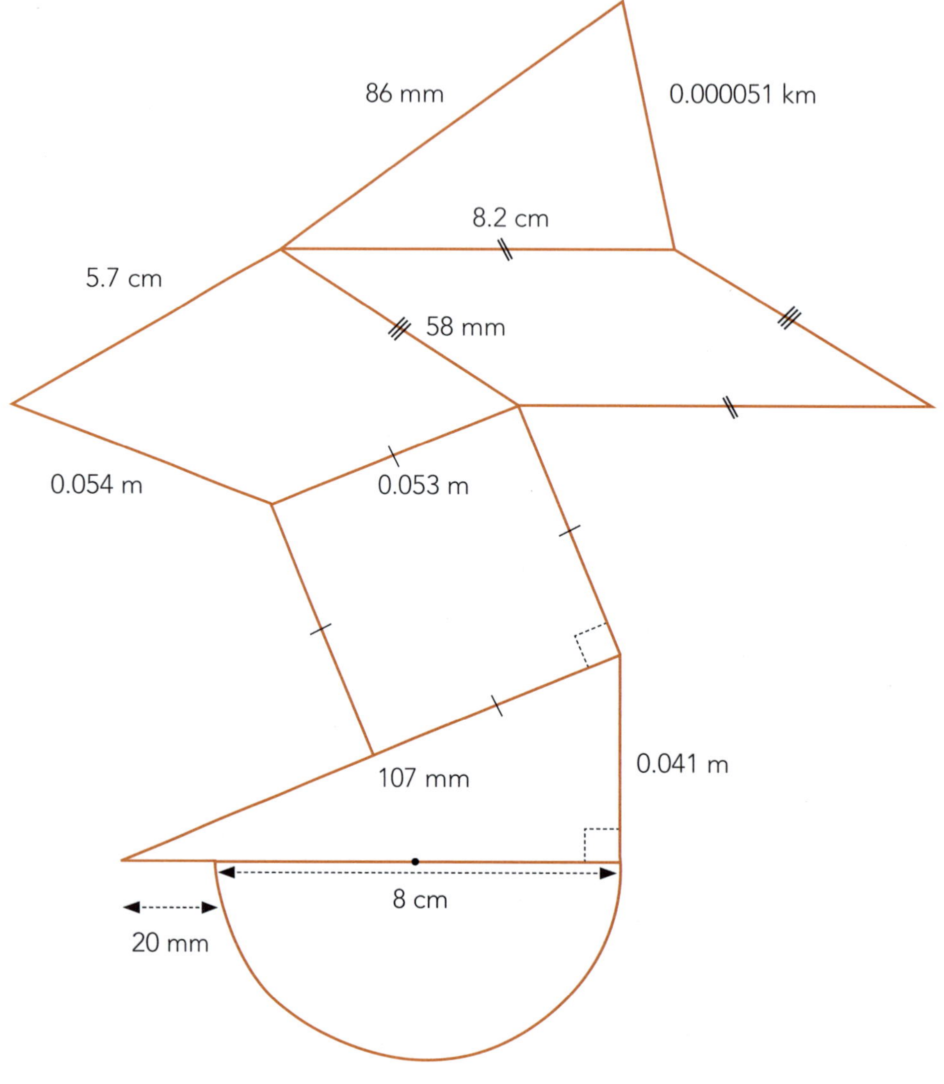

 ISBN: 9780170450454

Challenge 2

Answer the following questions.

1 Three books stand side by side in order: volumes I, II and III. Each volume is 4 cm thick. A bookworm starts outside the front cover of volume I and eats its way to the outside of the back cover of volume III. If it travels in a straight line, what distance does it cover?

2 In the Olympic 400 m hurdles race, there are ten equally spaced hurdles. There is 45 m before the first hurdle and 40 m after the last hurdle. What is the distance between the hurdles?

3 A rope ladder hangs over the side of a ship so the bottom rung just touches the surface. The rungs are 20 cm apart. If the tide comes in one metre, how many rungs will be under the water?

4 Each link in this anchor chain is 56 mm long. The links are 9 mm thick. What is the length of five links of chain?

56 mm

5 This parcel is 24 cm long, 16 cm deep and 18 cm high. The lengths needed for the bow and to attach the card total 40 cm. Calculate the total length of ribbon required.

6 There are three children in a family. The twins are the same height and their older brother is 5 cm taller. If their combined heights add to 4.7 m, how tall are the twins?

ISBN: 9780170450454

Area

Units of area

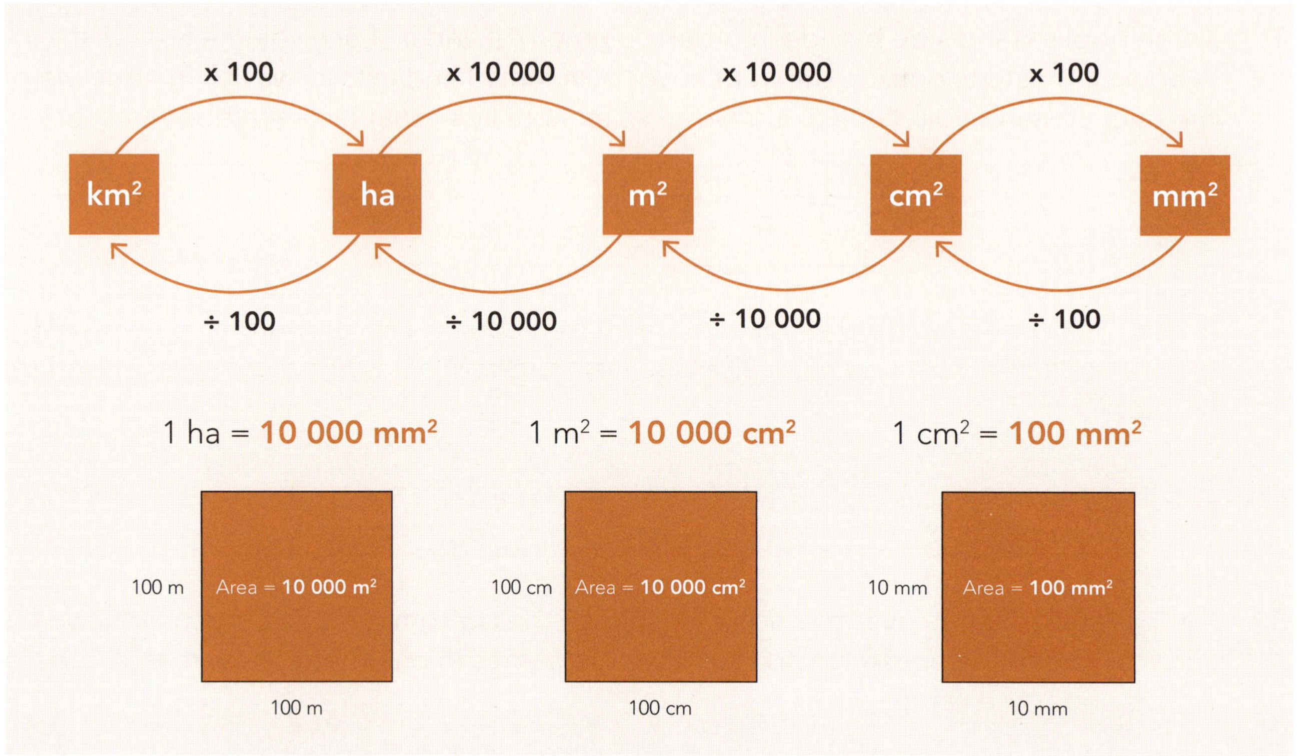

Highlight the correct conversion for each of the following.

1	6000 m^2	6 ha	0.6 ha
		0.006 ha	0.06 ha
3	95 000 mm^2	0.095 m^2	0.95 m^2
		95 cm^2	9500 cm^2
5	450 ha	4.5 km^2	0.45 km^2
		4500 m^2	0.045 km^2
7	101 000 cm^2	10.1 m^2	1.01 m^2
		0.101 m^2	101 m^2

2	7 ha	7000 m^2	0.07 km^2
		0.7 km^2	0.007 km^2
4	8100 cm^2	8.1 m^2	81 000 mm^2
		0.081 m^2	0.81 m^2
6	980 000 m^2	9.8 ha	98 ha
		0.098 km^2	980 ha
8	103 ha	1 030 000 m^2	103 000 m^2
		10 300 m^2	0.103 km^2

ISBN: 9780170450454

Quadrilaterals

Square and rectangle

> If you can **paint** it, it's area.

- The area is the size of a **flat surface** inside a two-dimensional (2D) shape.

Examples:

1

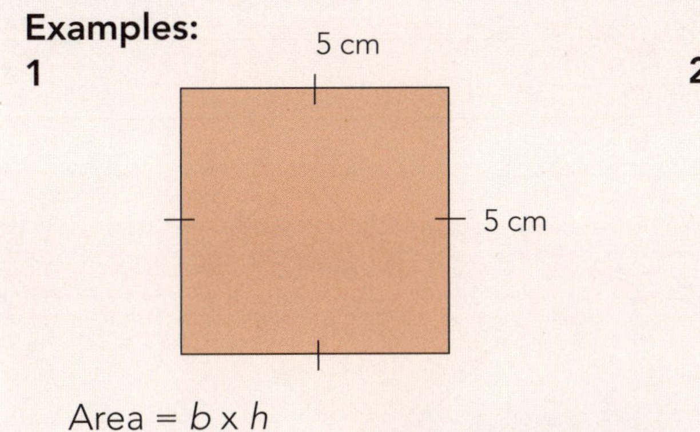

Area = $b \times h$
$= 5 \times 5$
$= 25\ \text{cm}^2$

> Units for area **must** be squared (^{2}).

2

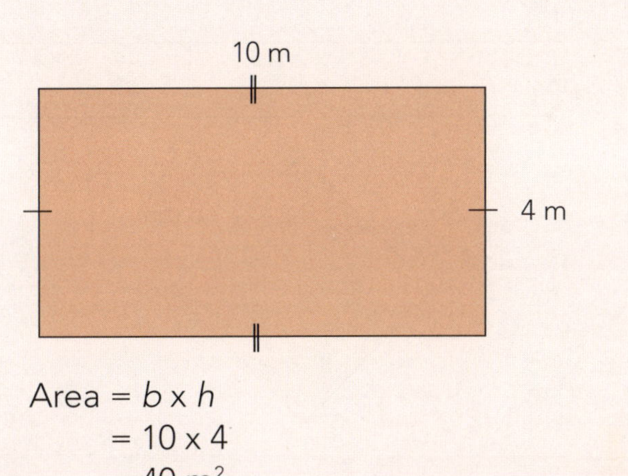

Area = $b \times h$
$= 10 \times 4$
$= 40\ \text{m}^2$

Calculate the areas of these squares and rectangles.

1

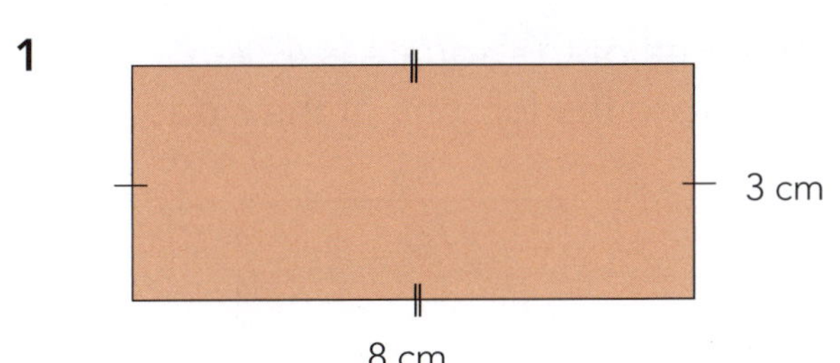

____

____

2

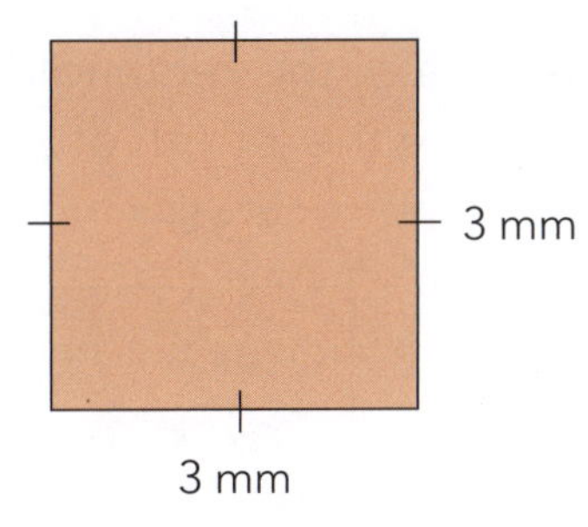

____

____

3

4 km

____

____

4

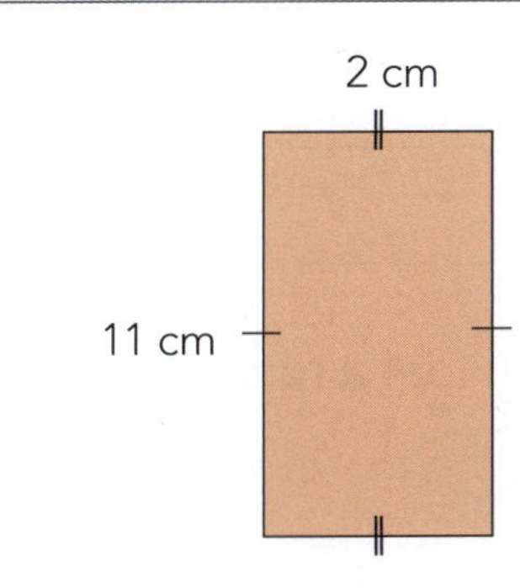

____

____

ISBN: 9780170450454

5 Write your answer in square centimetres (cm^2).

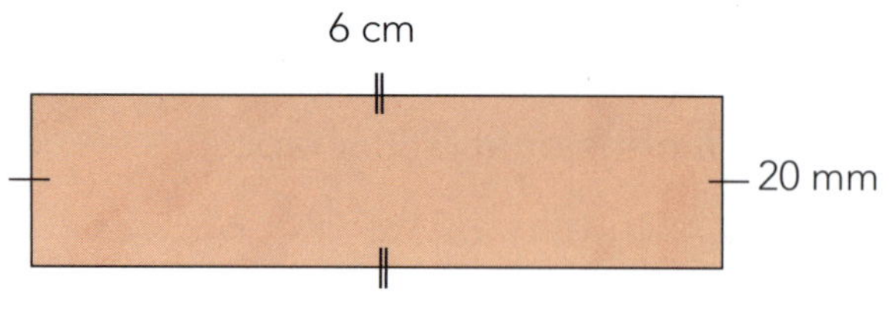

6 Write your answer in square metres (m^2).

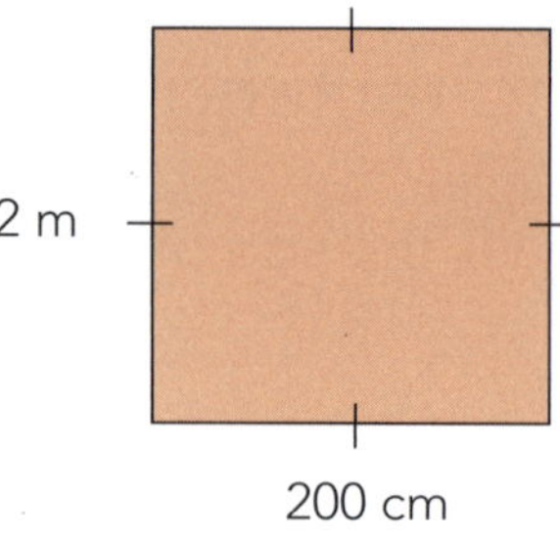

7

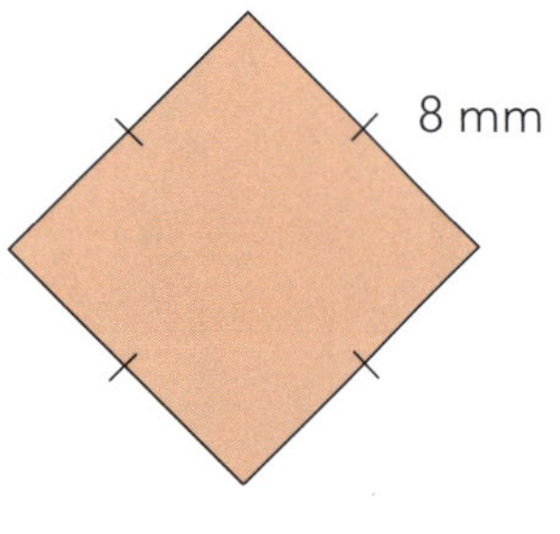

8

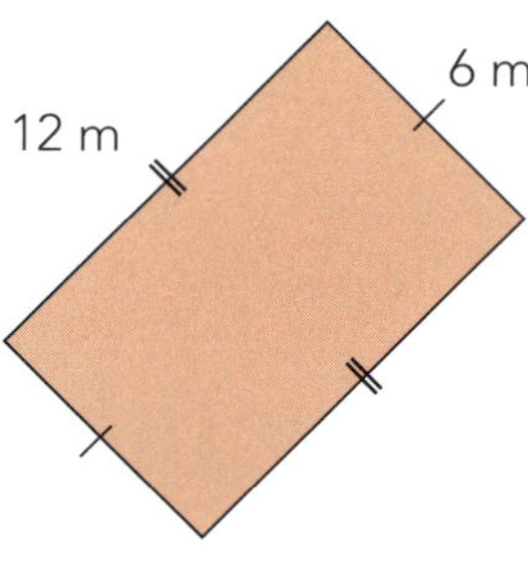

Answer the following questions.

9 The area of this rectangle is 18 km^2. Calculate the length of side h.

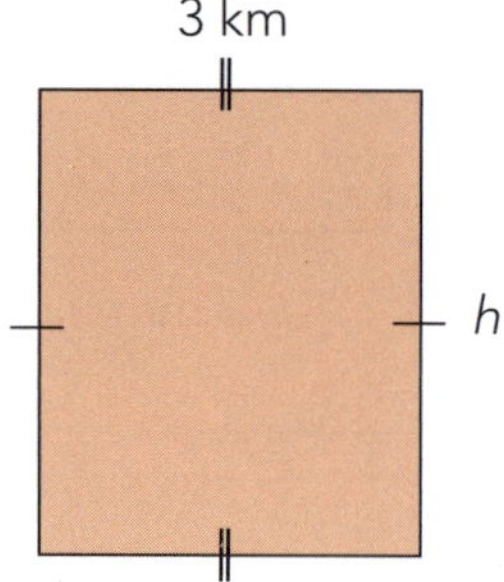

10 The area of this square is 49 cm^2. Calculate the lengths of the sides.

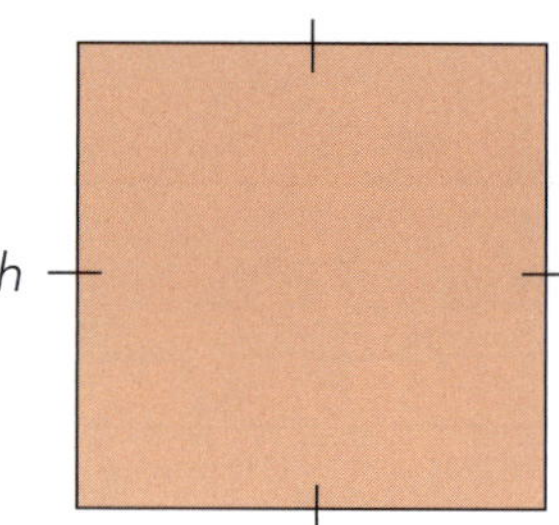

11 Sketch and label a rectangle with an area of 21 m^2.

12 Sketch and label a square with an area of 81 cm^2.

 ISBN: 9780170450454

Parallelogram and rhombus

- A **parallelogram** has opposite sides that are parallel and equal.
- A **rhombus** has four equal sides, and opposite sides are parallel.

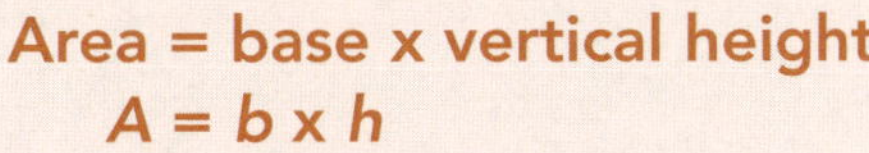

Examples:

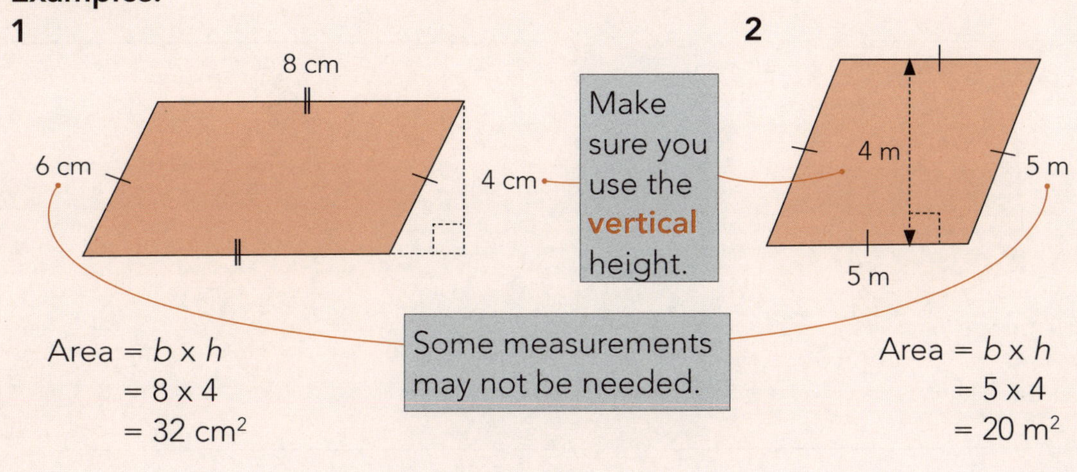

Area = $b \times h$
= 8×4
= $32\ \text{cm}^2$

Area = $b \times h$
= 5×4
= $20\ \text{m}^2$

Calculate the areas of these shapes.

1

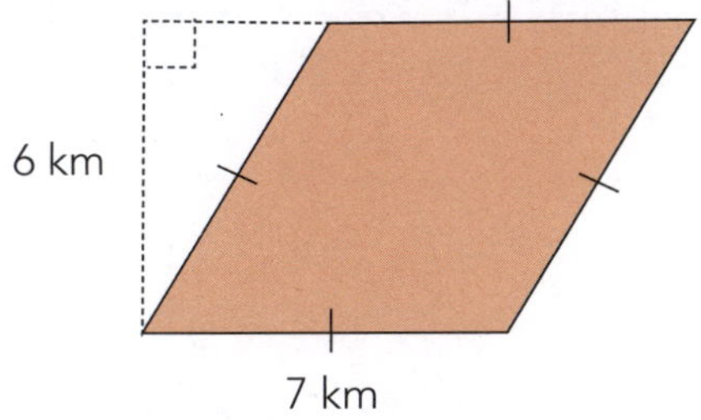

2

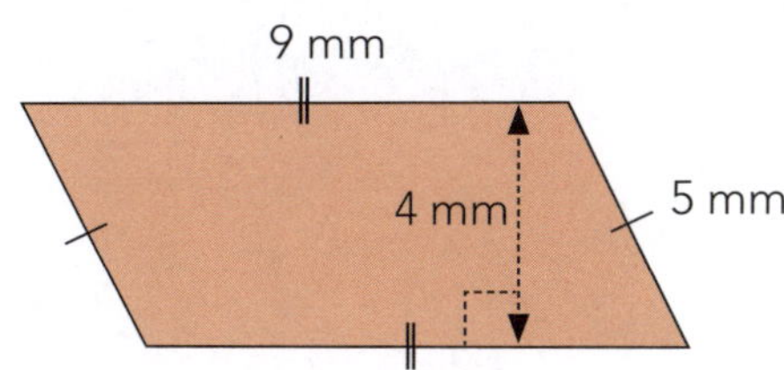

3

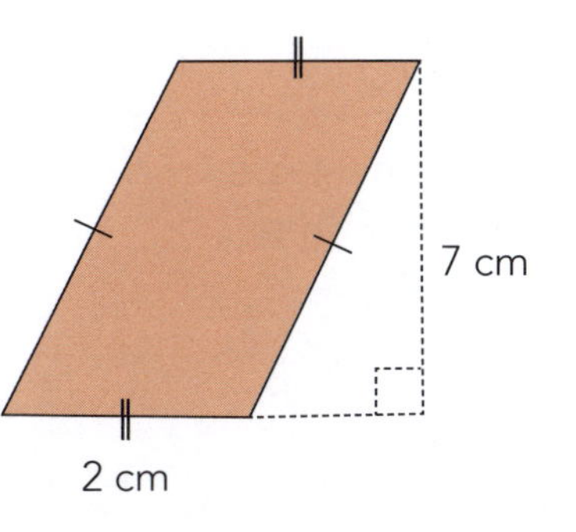

4

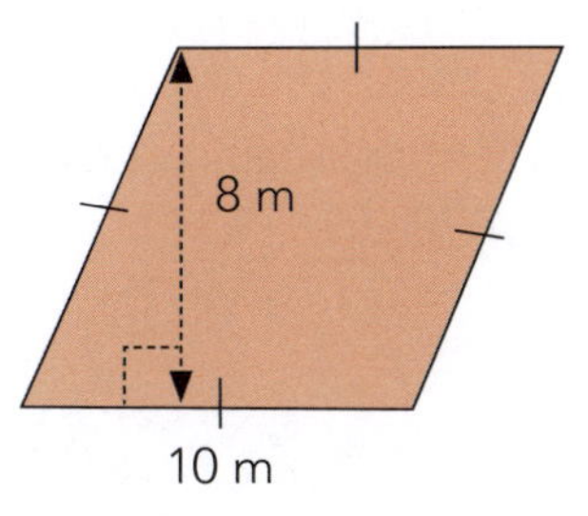

5

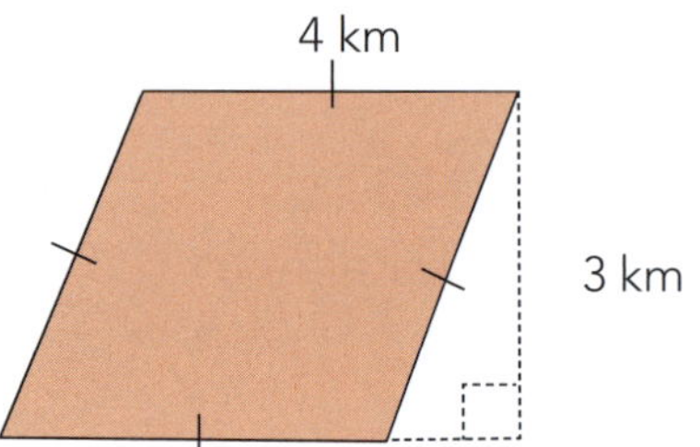

6

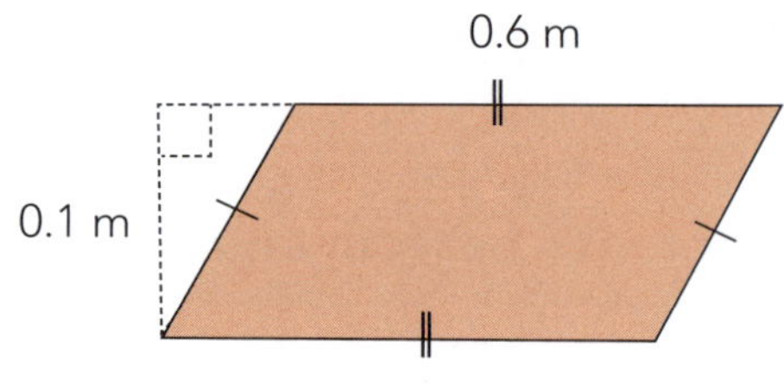

7

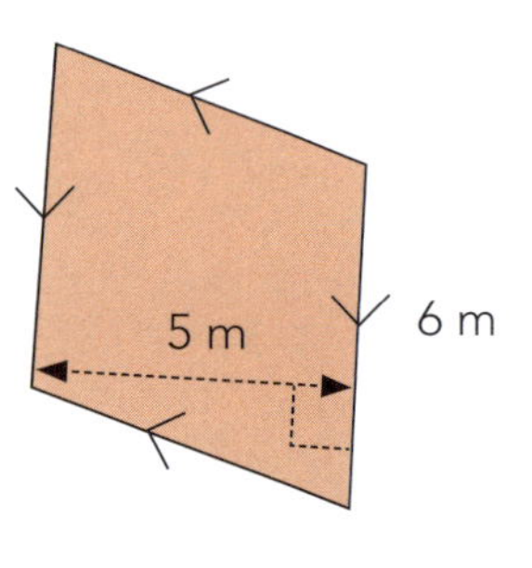

8

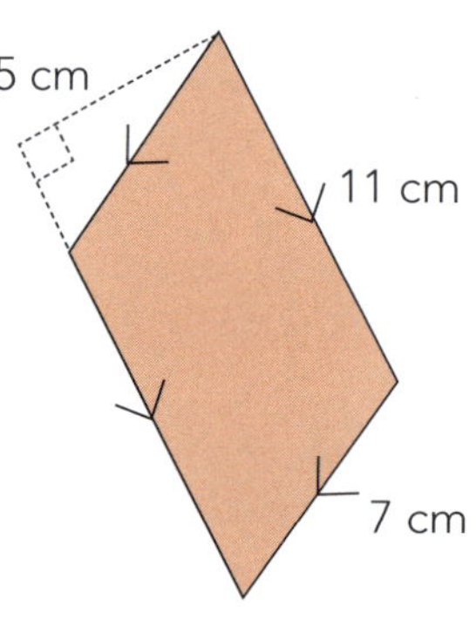

9 The area of this parallelogram is 63 cm². Calculate the length of *h*.

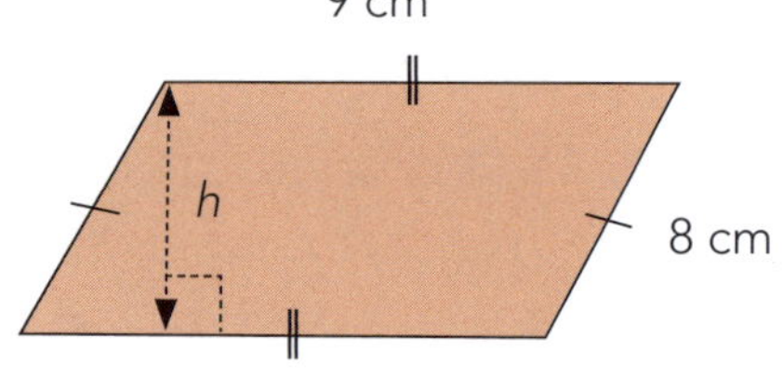

10 The area of this rhombus is 72 m². Calculate the length of the sides.

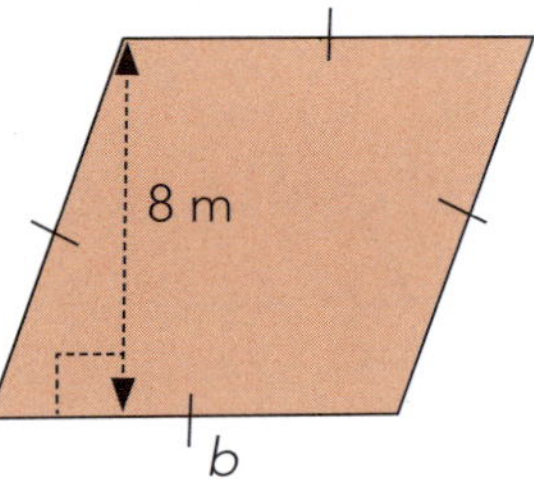

Answer the following questions.

11 Sketch and label a rhombus with an area of 30 cm².

12 Sketch and label a parallelogram with an area of 48 m².

 ISBN: 9780170450454

Trapezium

- A **trapezium** has two parallel sides; the other two sides are not parallel.

Area = (average of *a* and *b*) x vertical height

$$A = \frac{a + b}{2} \times h$$

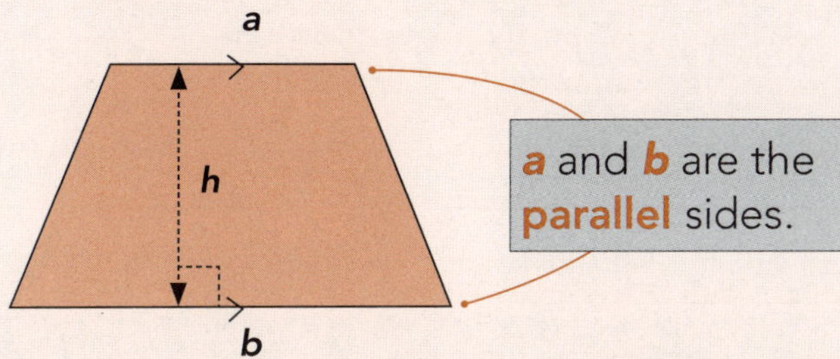

Examples:

1

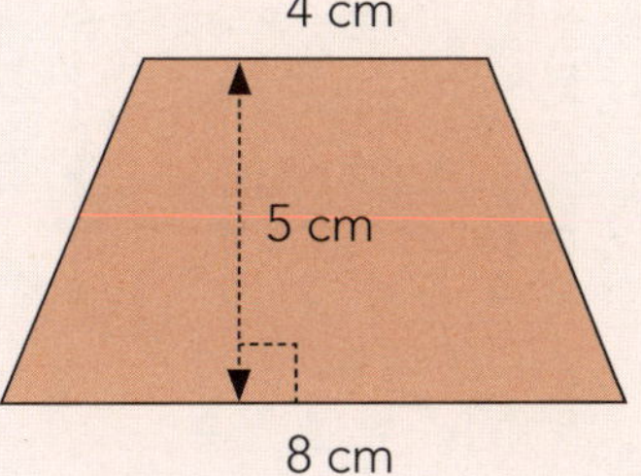

$$\text{Area} = \frac{a + b}{2} \times h$$
$$= \frac{4 + 8}{2} \times 5$$
$$= 30 \text{ cm}^2$$

2

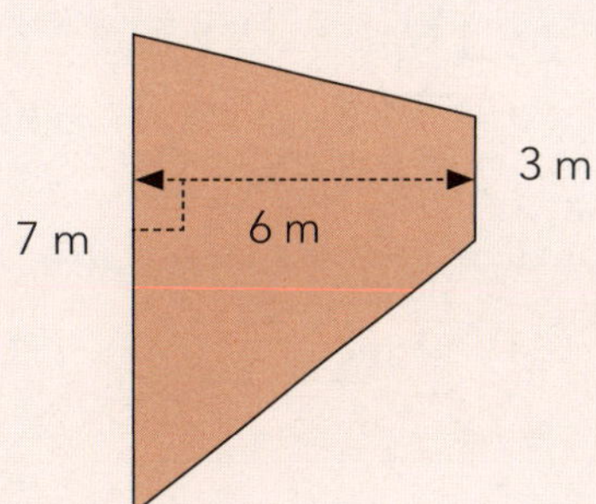

$$\text{Area} = \frac{a + b}{2} \times h$$
$$= \frac{7 + 3}{2} \times 6$$
$$= 30 \text{ m}^2$$

Calculate the areas of these shapes.

1

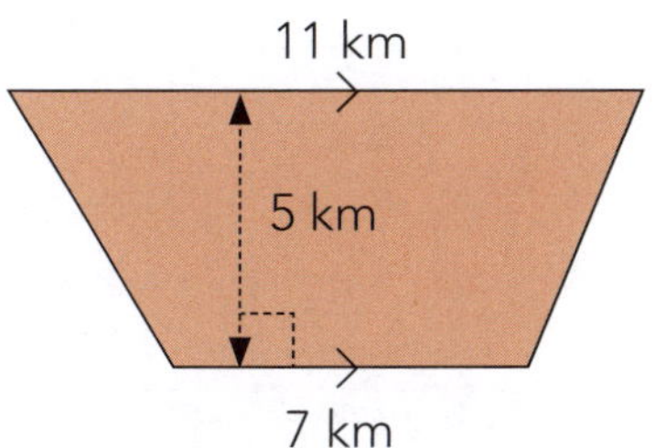

____

____

2

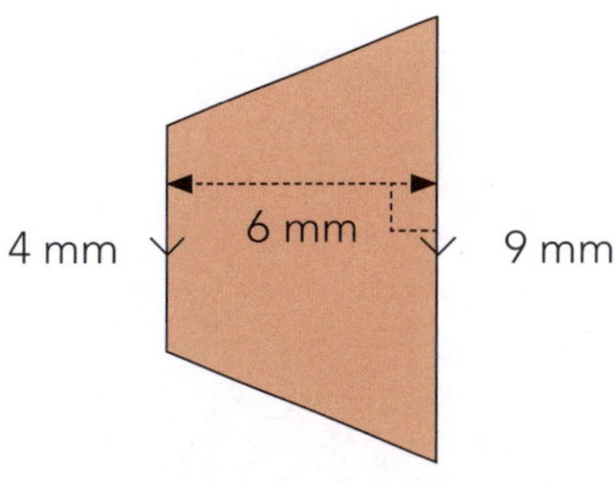

____

____

3

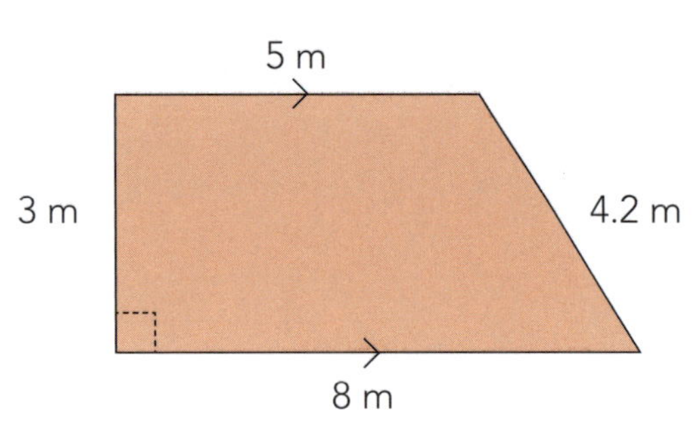

4

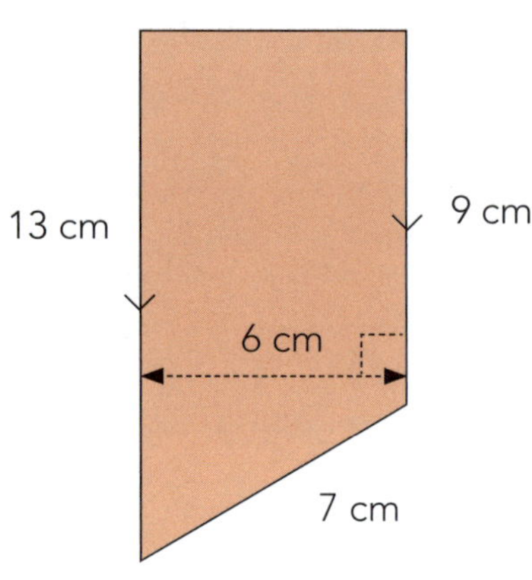

5

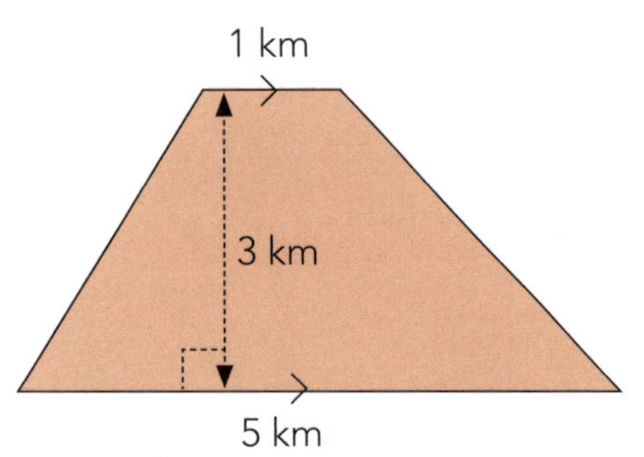

6

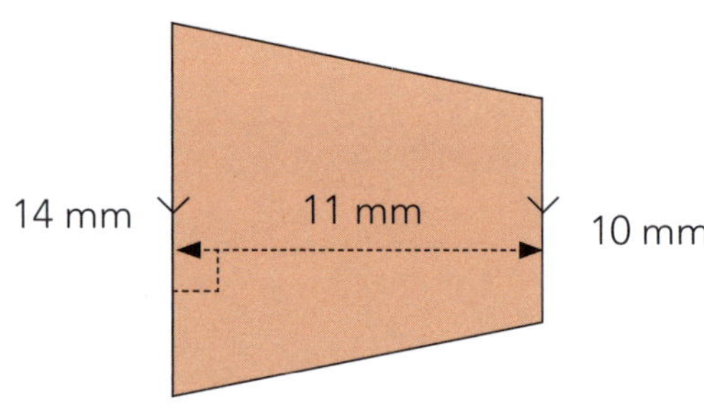

Calculate the areas of these shapes.

7 The area of this trapezium is 42 m^2. Calculate the length of side x.

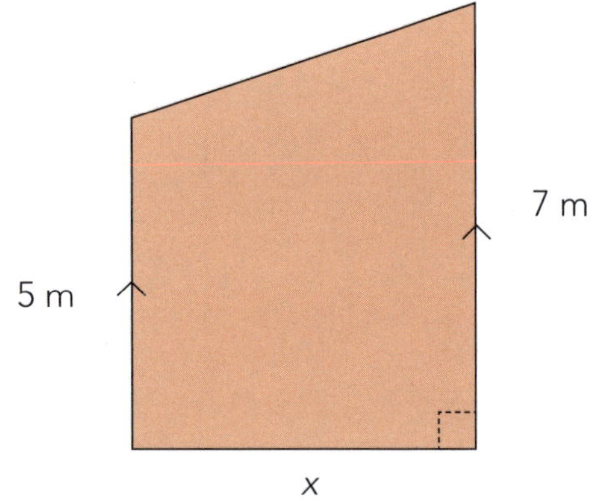

8 The area of this trapezium is 38.5 km^2. Calculate the length of side x.

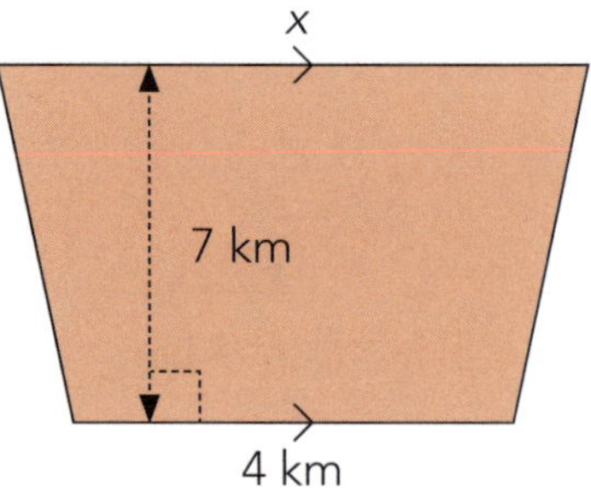

 ISBN: 9780170450454

Triangles

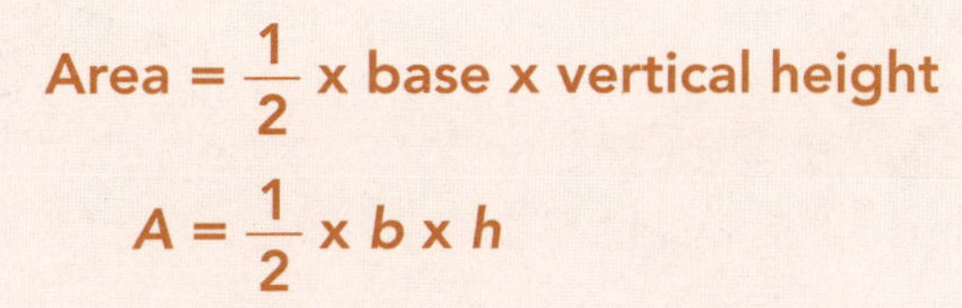

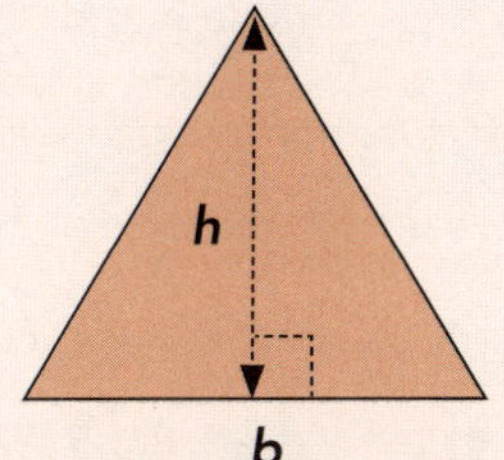

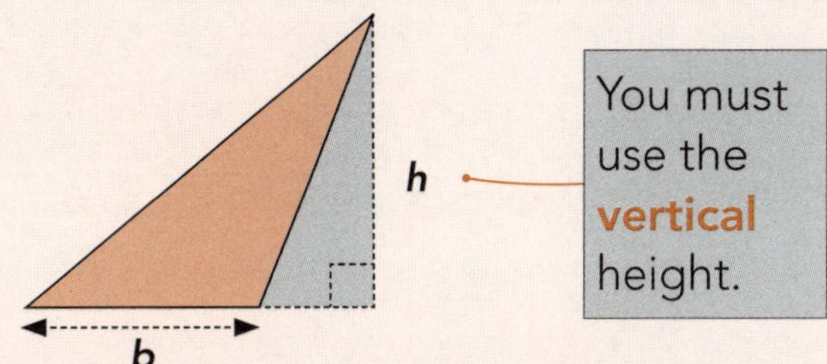

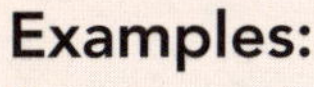

1

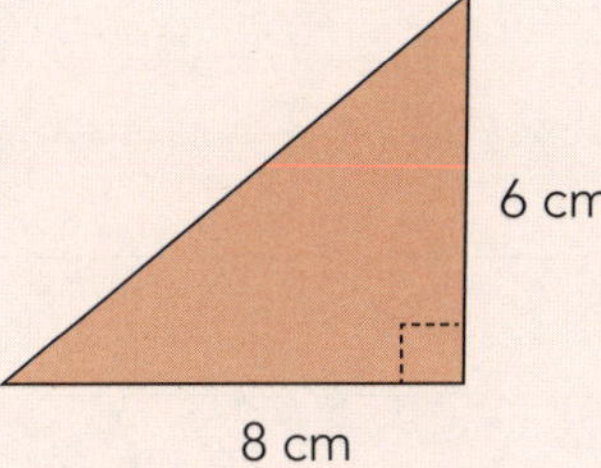

$$\text{Area} = \frac{1}{2} \times b \times h$$
$$= \frac{1}{2} \times 8 \times 6$$
$$= 24 \text{ cm}^2$$

2

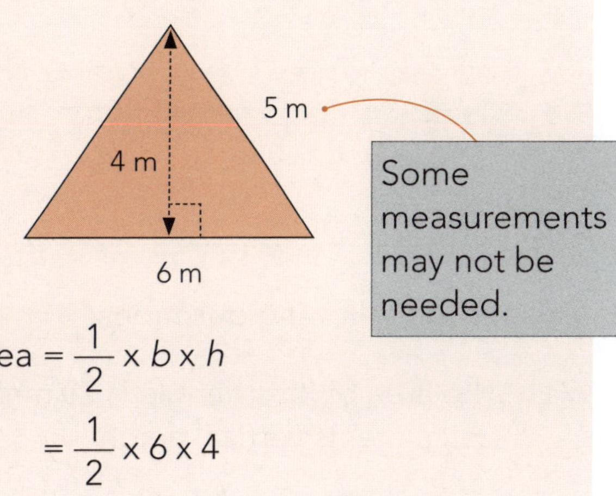

$$\text{Area} = \frac{1}{2} \times b \times h$$
$$= \frac{1}{2} \times 6 \times 4$$
$$= 12 \text{ m}^2$$

Calculate the areas of these shapes.

1

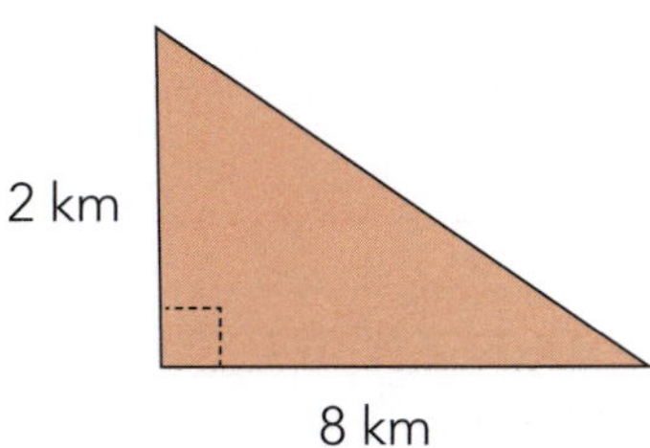

____

____

2

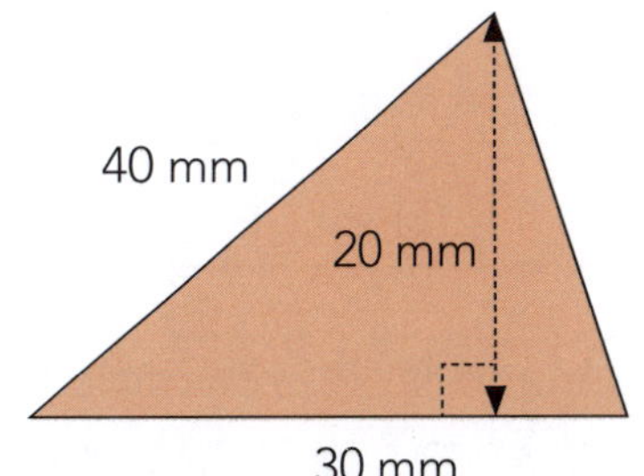

____

____

ISBN: 9780170450454

3

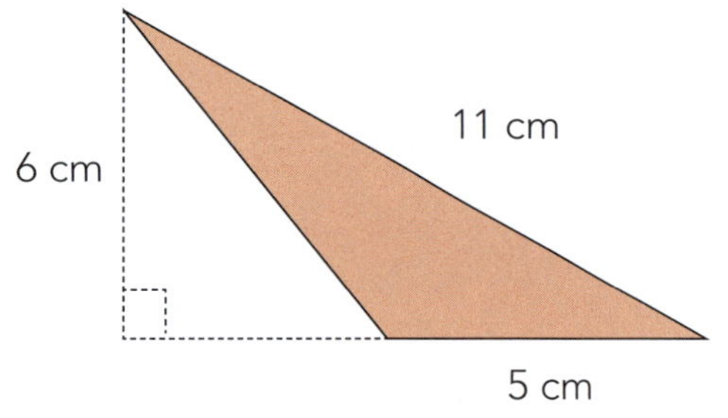

4

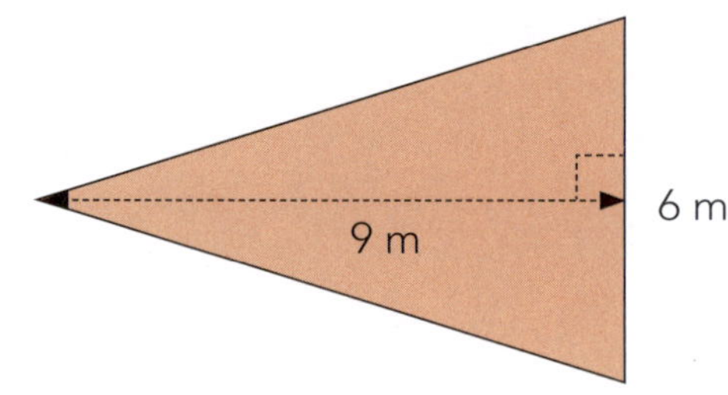

5

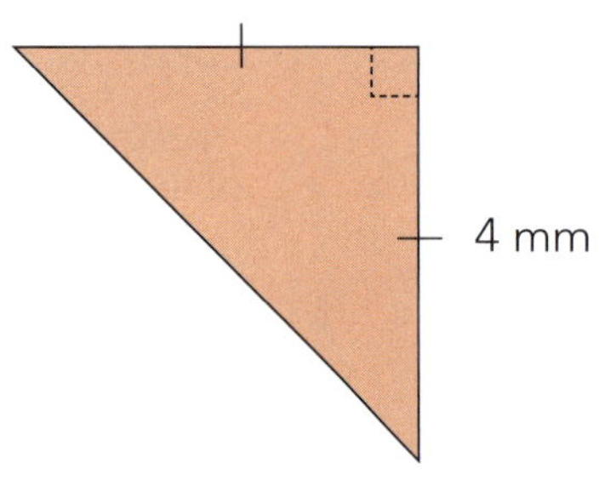

6

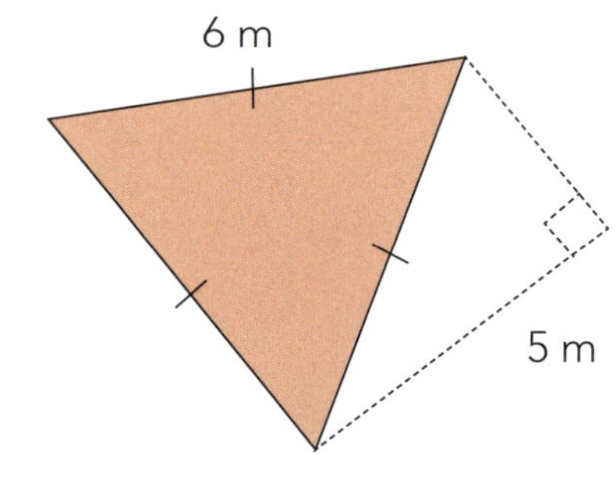

Answer the following questions.

7 The area of this triangle is 28 mm^2. Calculate its vertical height, h.

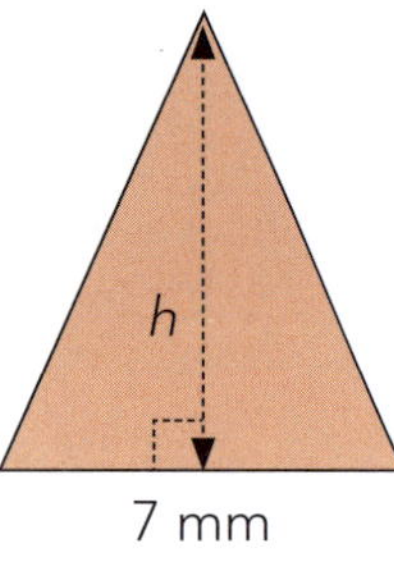

8 The area of this triangle is 66 cm^2. Calculate the length of its base, b.

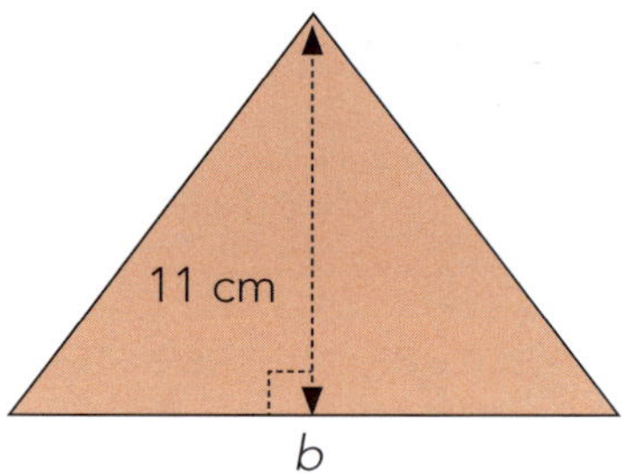

9 Sketch and label a triangle with an area of 24 m^2.

10 Sketch and label a triangle with an area of 900 mm^2.

ISBN: 9780170450454

Circles

Area = π x radius^2

$$A = \pi r^2$$

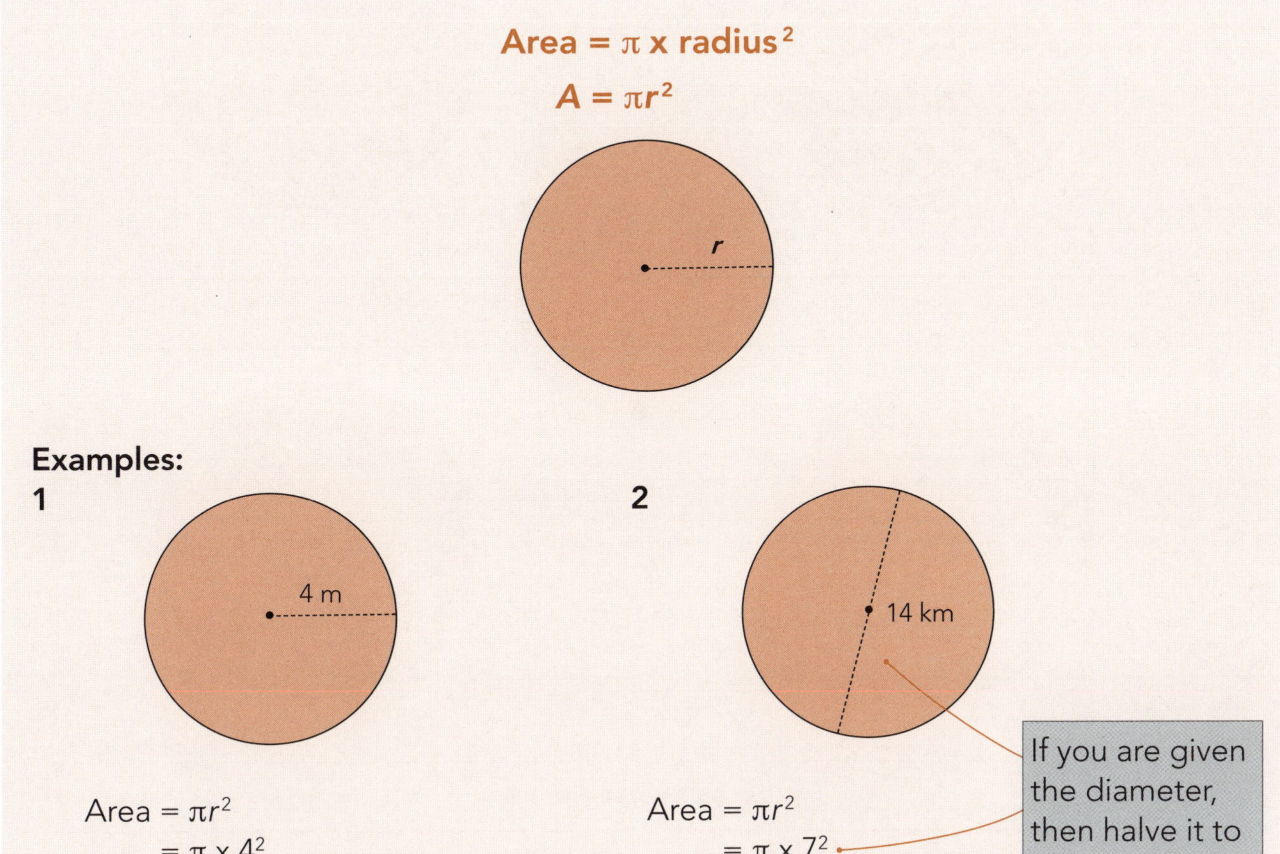

Examples:

1

Area = πr^2
= $\pi \times 4^2$
= 50.27 m^2 (2 dp)

2

Area = πr^2
= $\pi \times 7^2$
= 153.94 km^2 (2 dp)

Calculate the areas of these circles.

1

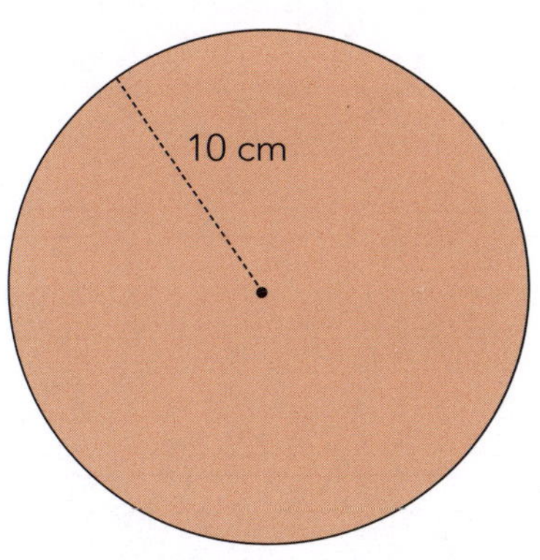

____

____

2

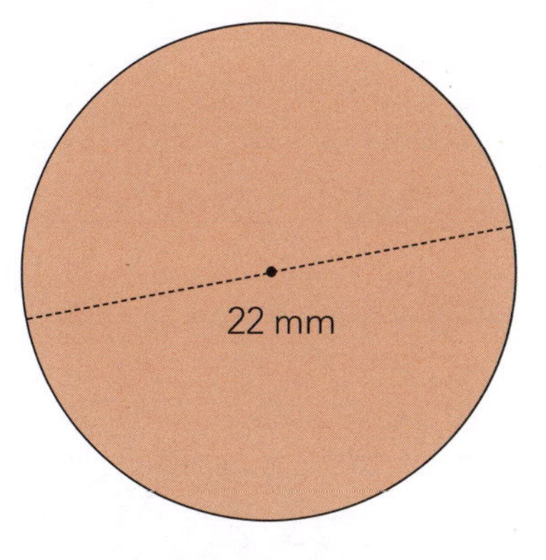

____

____

ISBN: 9780170450454

3

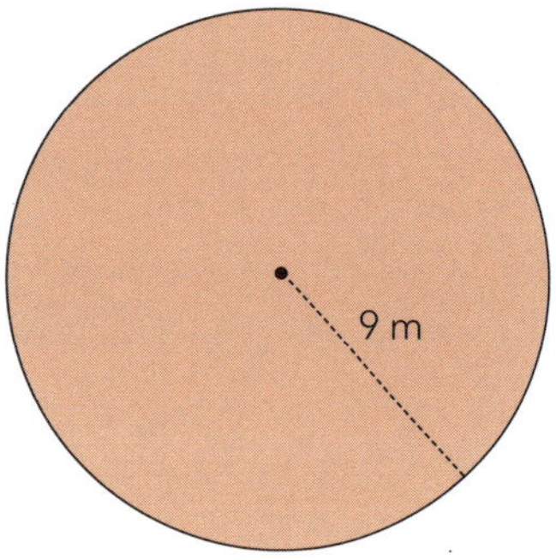

9 m

4

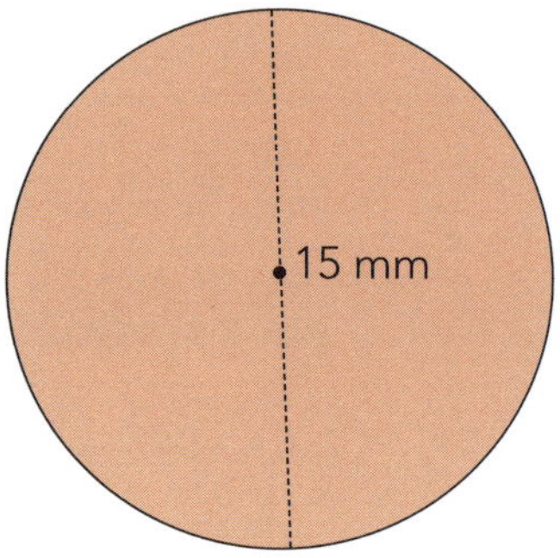

15 mm

5

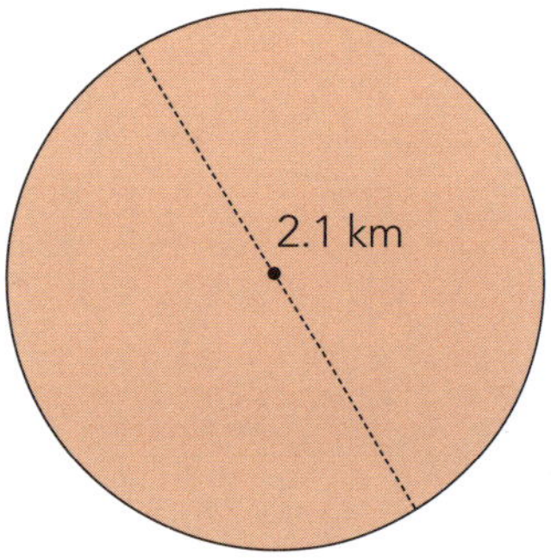

2.1 km

6

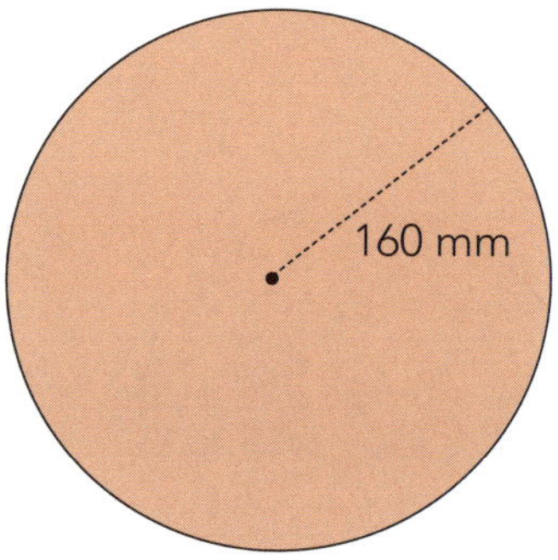

160 mm

7

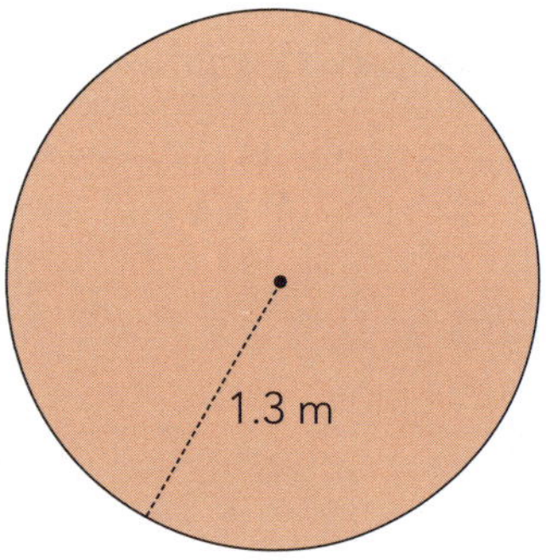

1.3 m

8

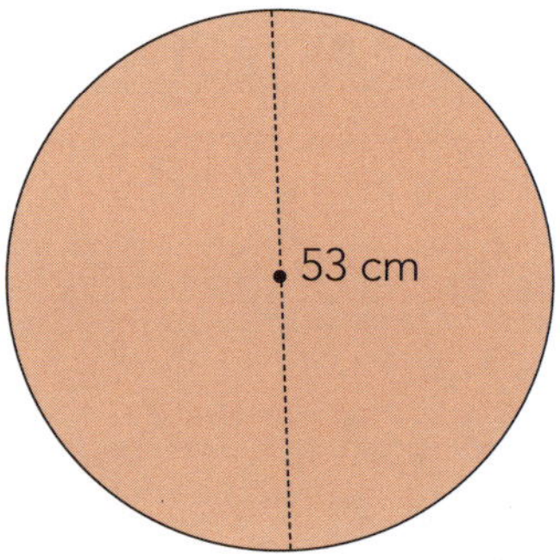

53 cm

9

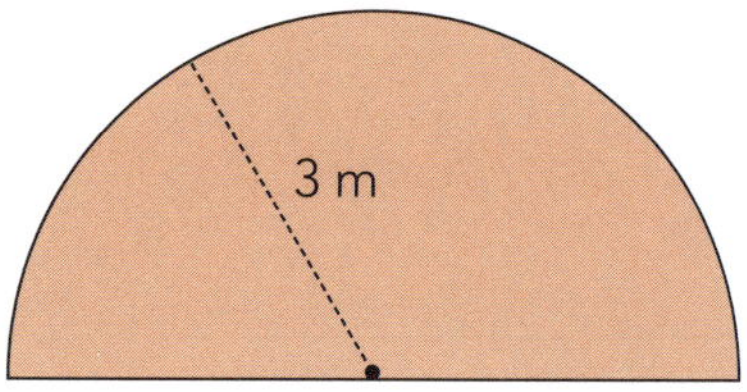

3 m

10

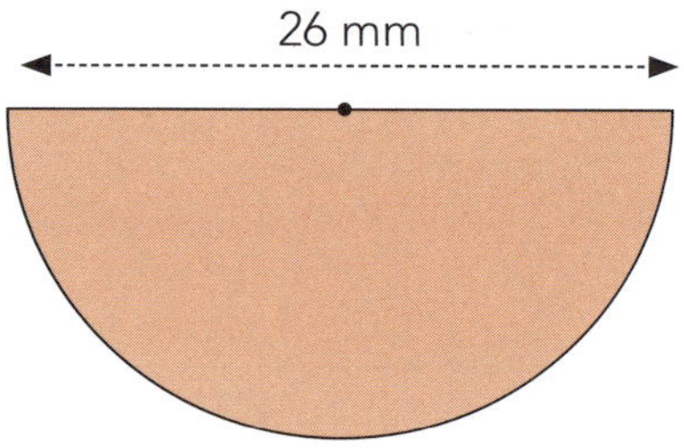

26 mm

 ISBN: 9780170450454

11

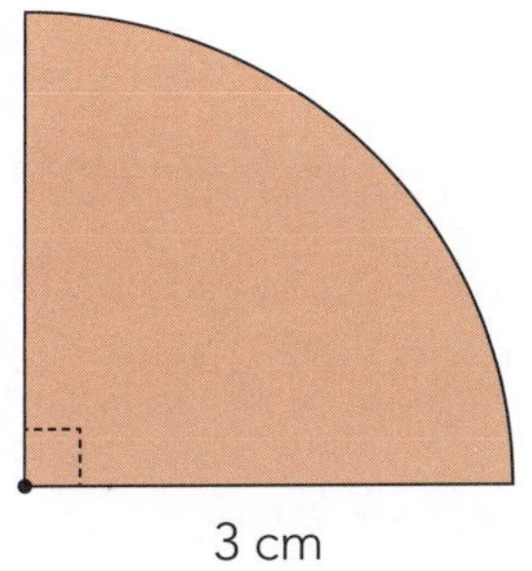

12

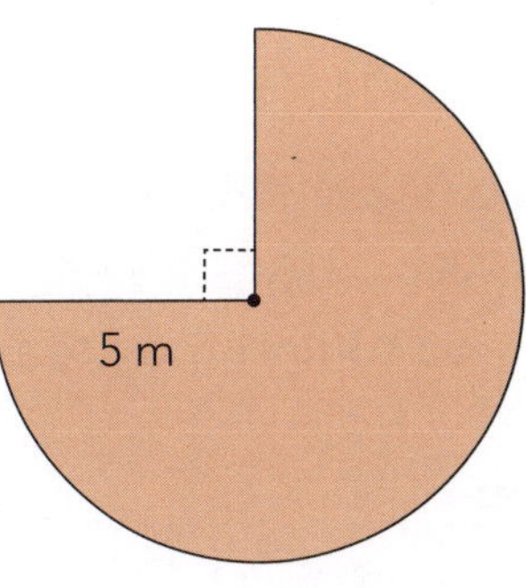

Answer the following questions.

13 The area of this circle is 706.86 km^2 (2 dp). Calculate the length of its radius, *r*.

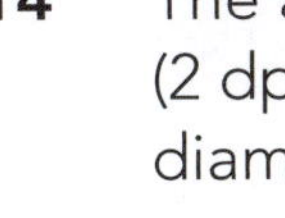

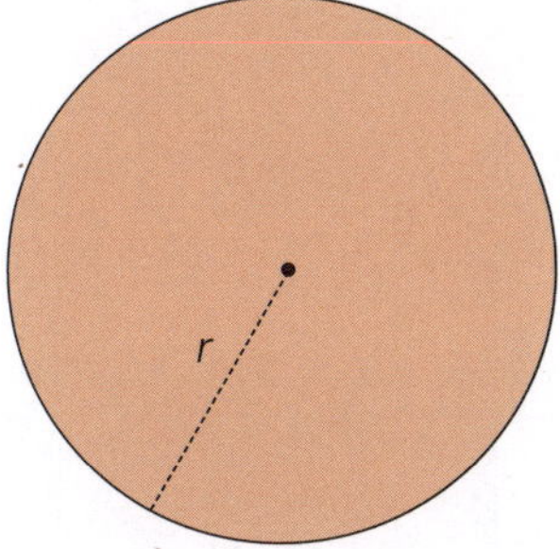

14 The area of this circle is 1661.90 m^2 (2 dp). Calculate the length of its diameter, *d*.

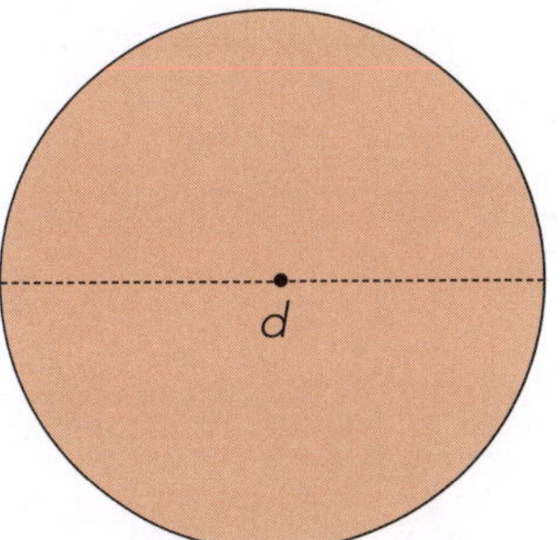

15 The area of the semicircle is 52.84 cm^2 (2 dp). Calculate the length of its radius, *r*.

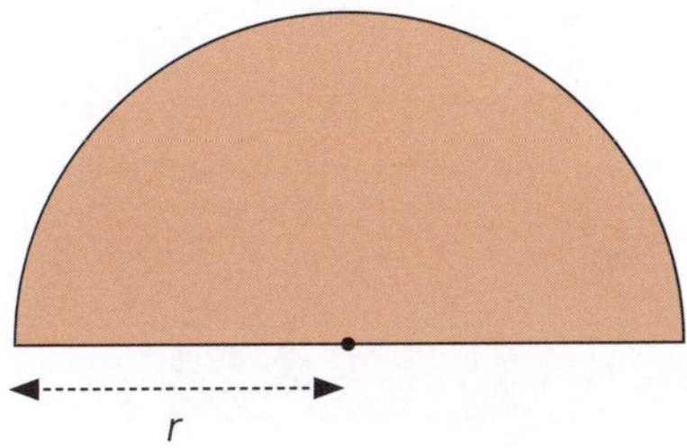

16 The area of the semicircle is 41 990.92 mm^2 (2 dp). Calculate the length of its diameter, *d*.

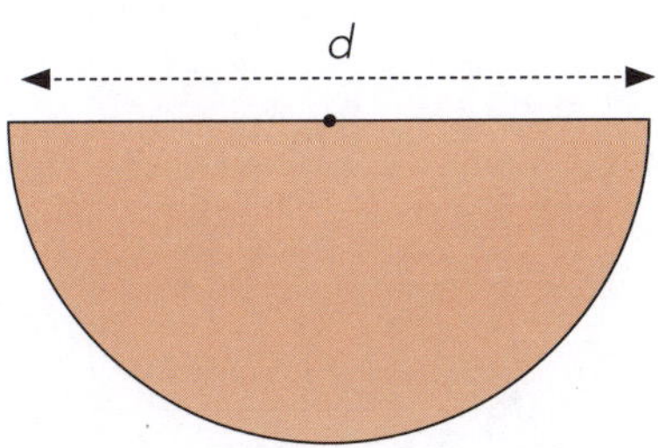

ISBN: 9780170450454

Compound shapes

- Remember, compound shapes are shapes that are made up of **other simple shapes**.
- You need to find the areas of the simple shapes and then **add** them together.

Example:

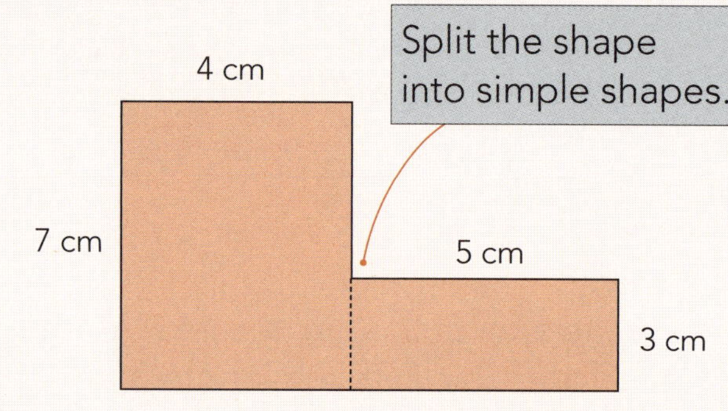

$$\text{Area} = (b_1 \times h_1) + (b_2 \times h_2)$$
$$= (4 \times 7) + (5 \times 3)$$
$$= 28 + 15$$
$$= 43\ \text{cm}^2$$

Calculate the two areas and add them together.

Calculate the areas of these shapes.

1

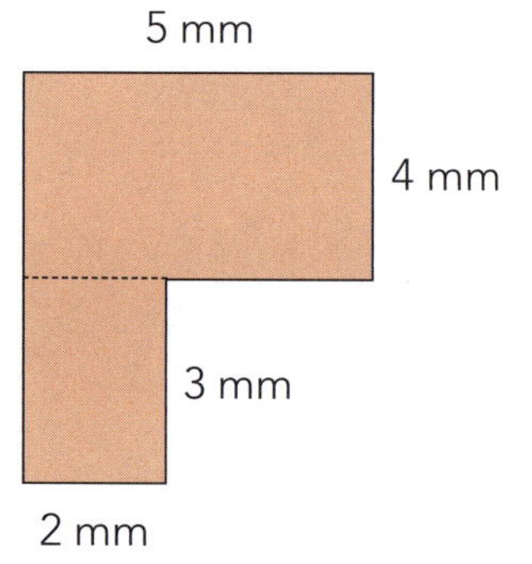

2

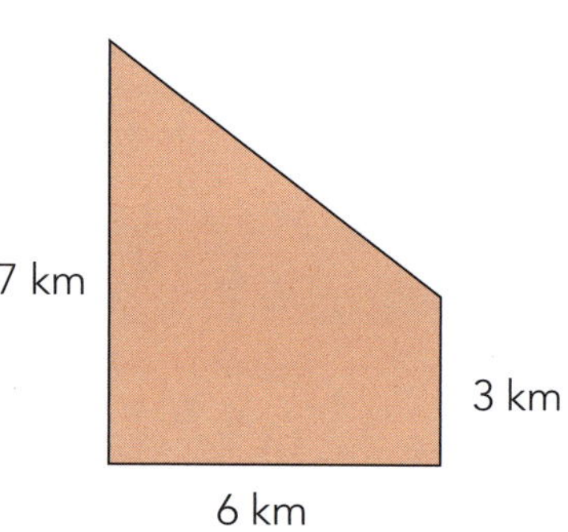

3

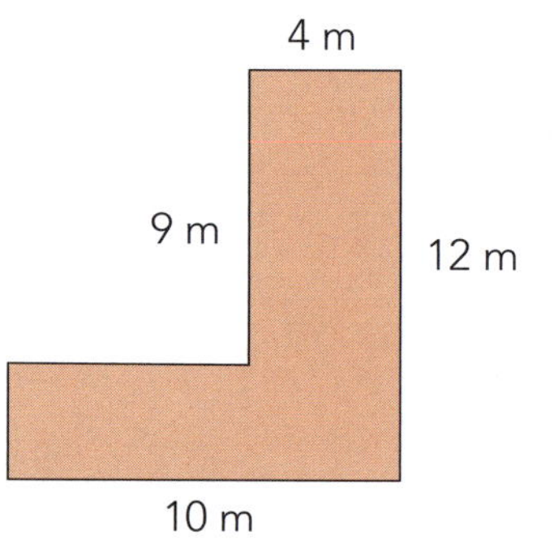

4

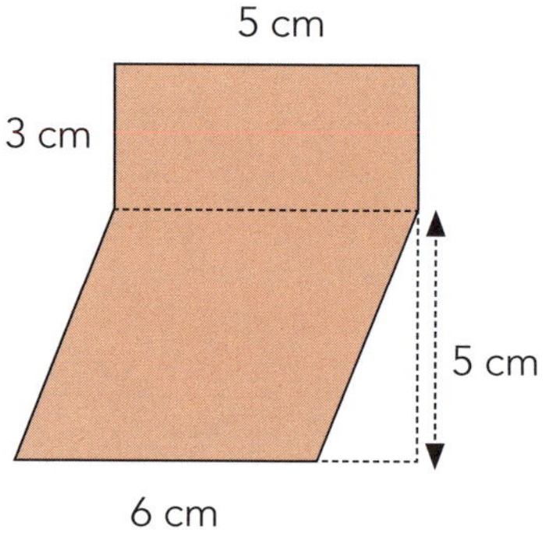

ISBN: 9780170450454

5

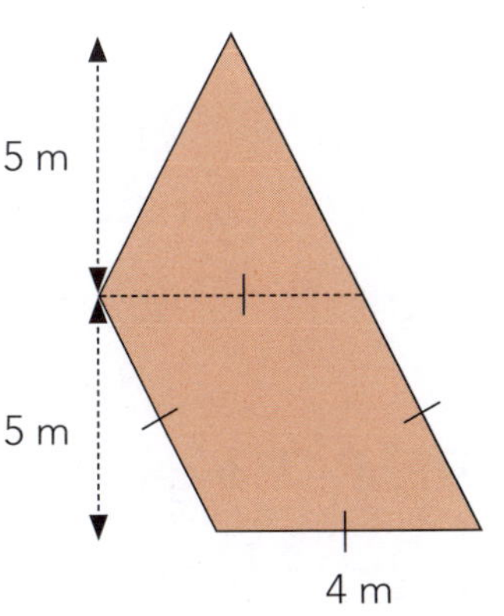

6

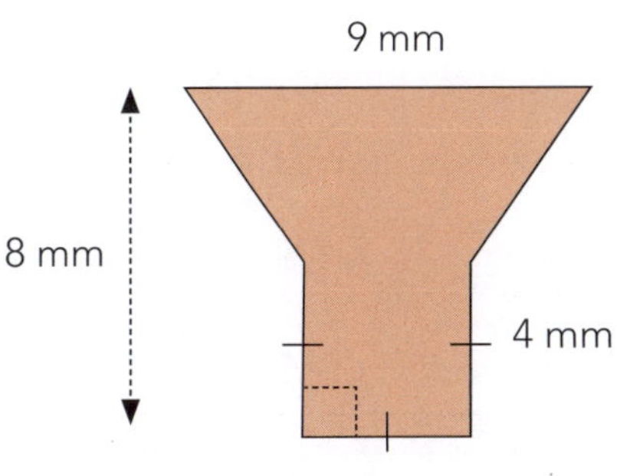

7

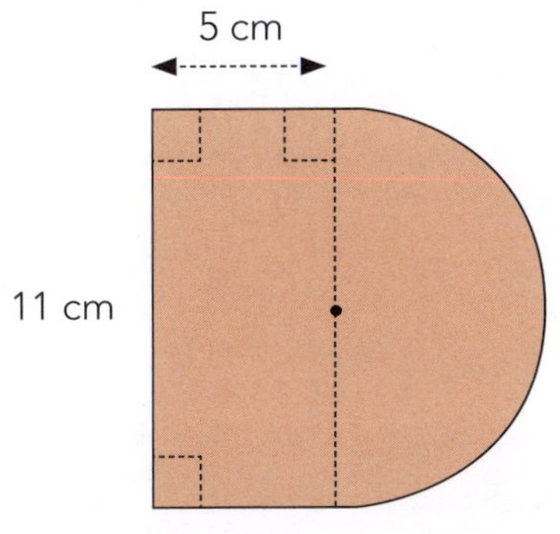

8

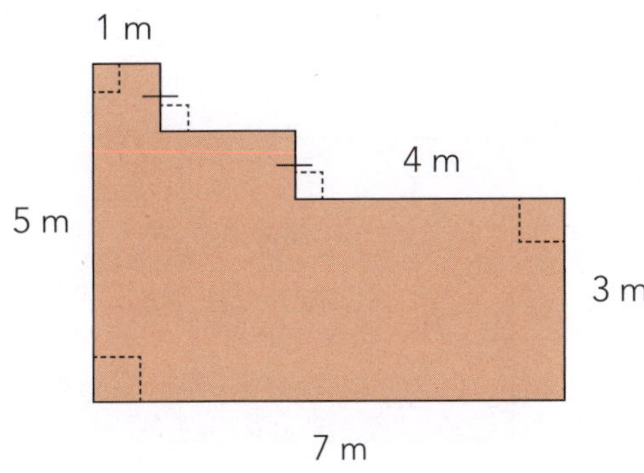

9

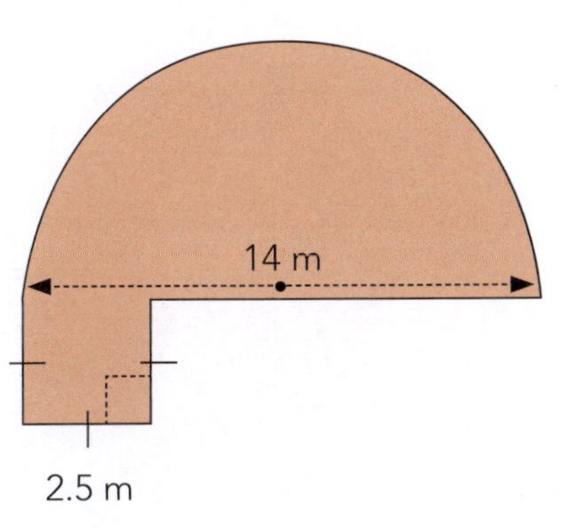

10

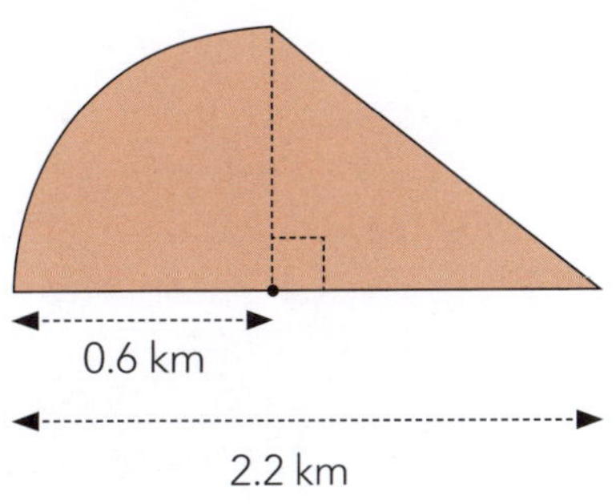

Shapes with holes

- You need to find the areas of the simple shapes and then **subtract** one from the other.

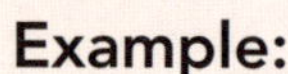

Example:

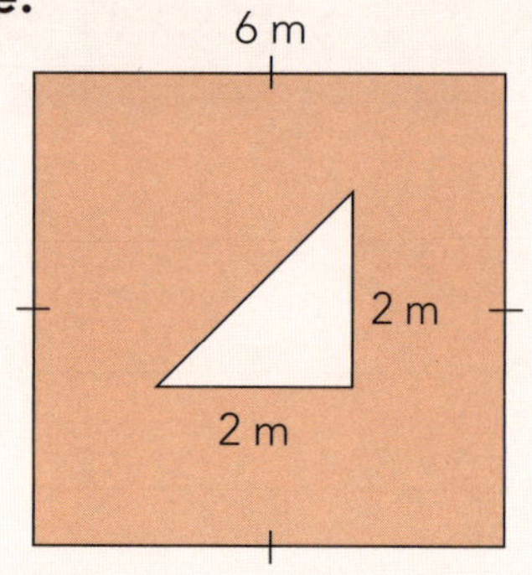

Shaded area = square – triangle

$= (6 \times 6) - (\frac{1}{2} \times 2 \times 2)$

$= 36 - 2$

$= 34 \text{ m}^2$

Calculate the two areas and subtract one from the other.

Calculate the shaded areas of these shapes.

1

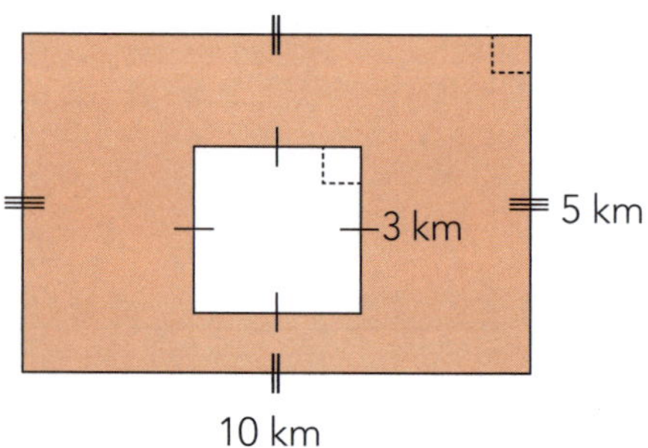

2

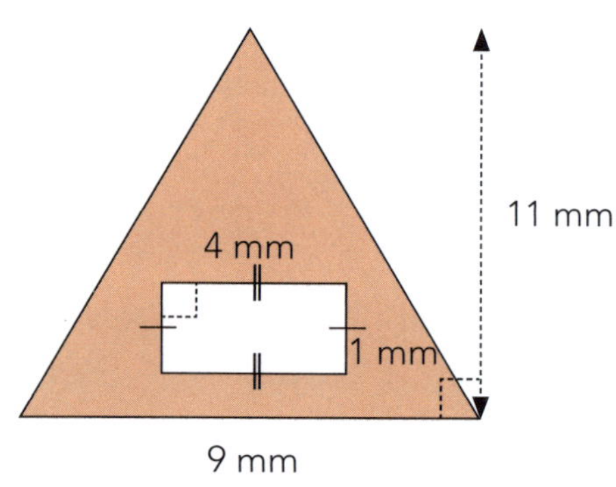

3

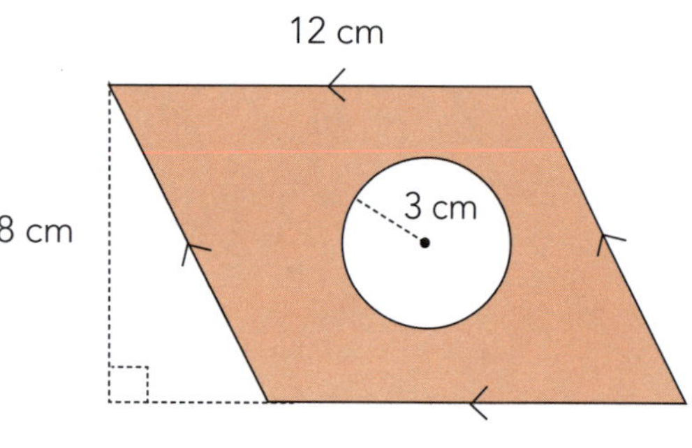

4

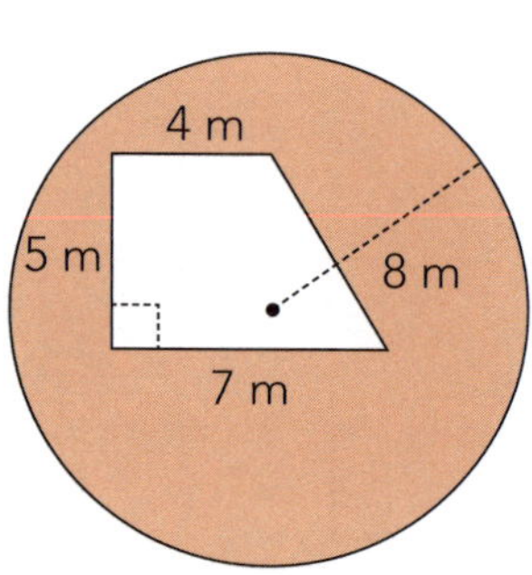

 ISBN: 9780170450454

5

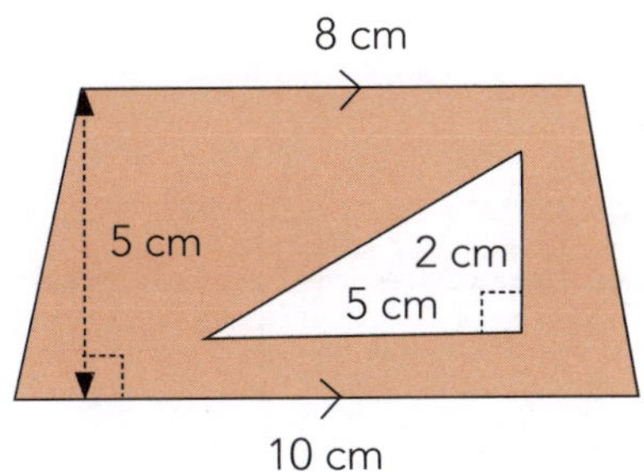

6 This diagram is composed of rectangles.

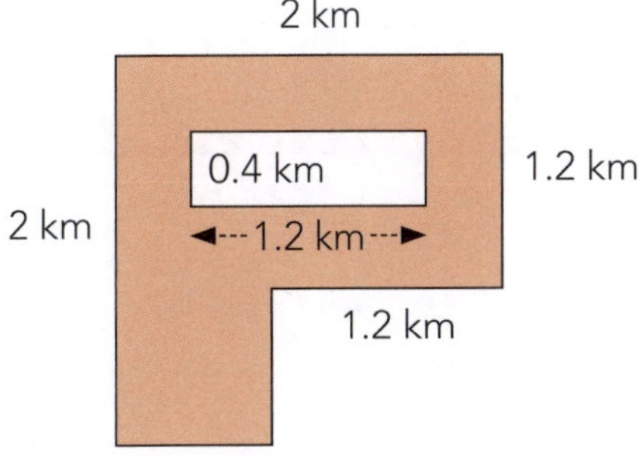

7

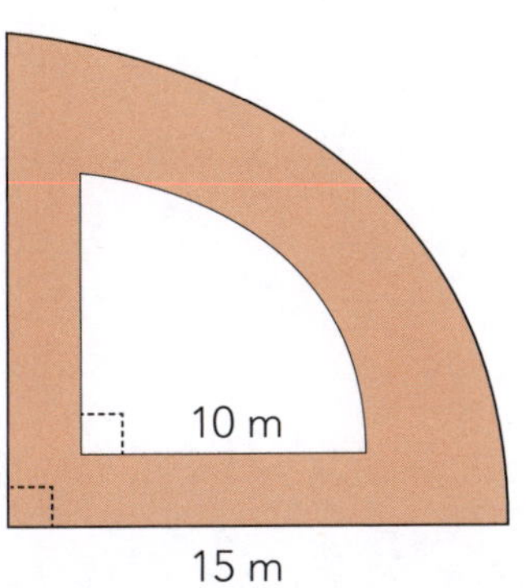

8 The larger shape is a rhombus.

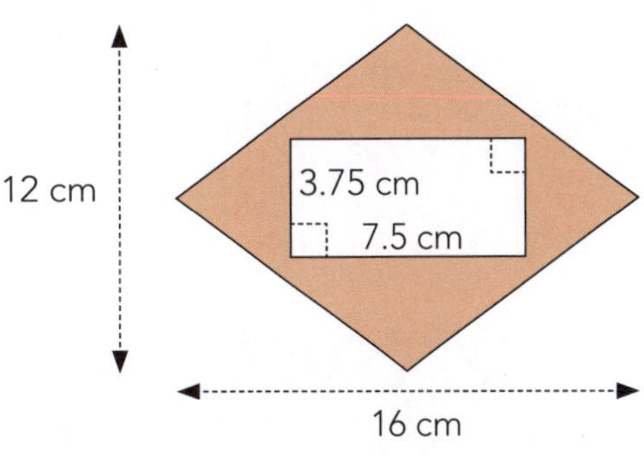

9 This is a regular pentagon with a square removed.

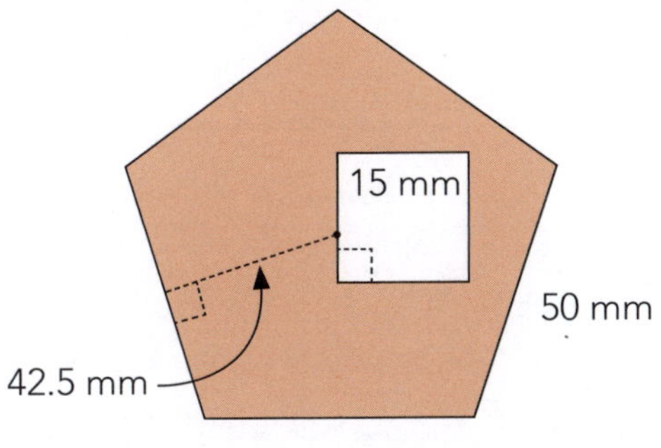

10 A shaded rectangle has an unshaded circular hole in the middle. The sides of the rectangle are 12 km and 9.5 km. The circle has a diameter of 5.5 km.

Summary

Complete the table.

Shape	Picture	Formula
Quadrilateral (square, rectangle, parallelogram, rhombus)	height base	$A = b \times h$
Trapezium		
Triangle		
Circle		

 ISBN: 9780170450454

Mixing it up

Calculate the areas of these shapes.

1

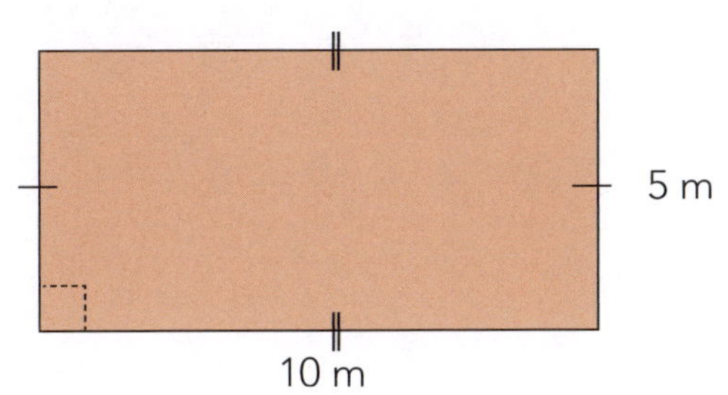

2

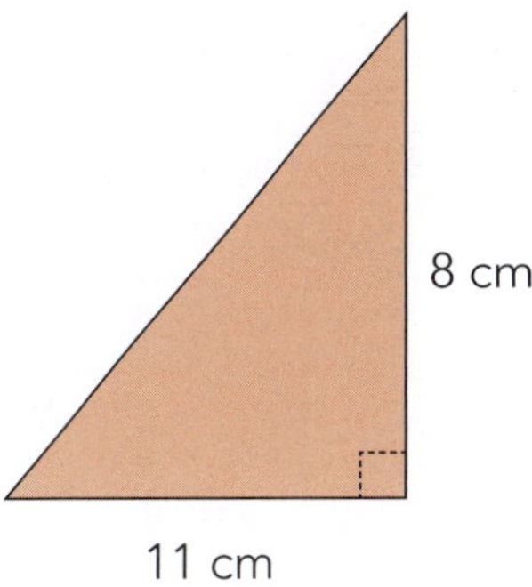

3

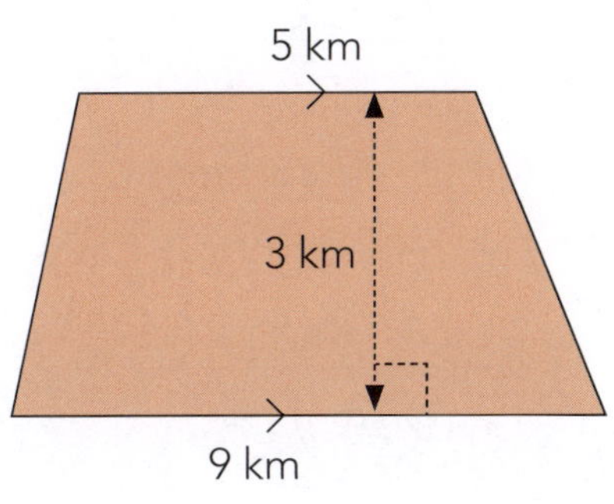

4

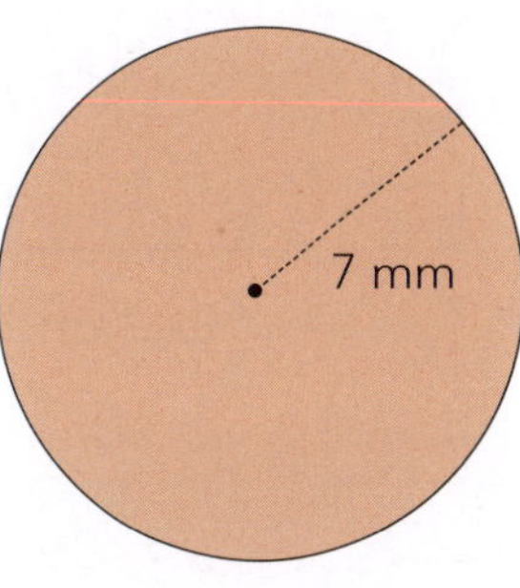

5

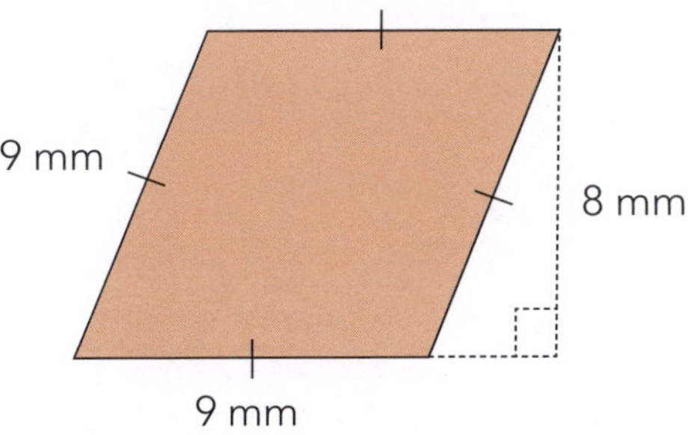

6

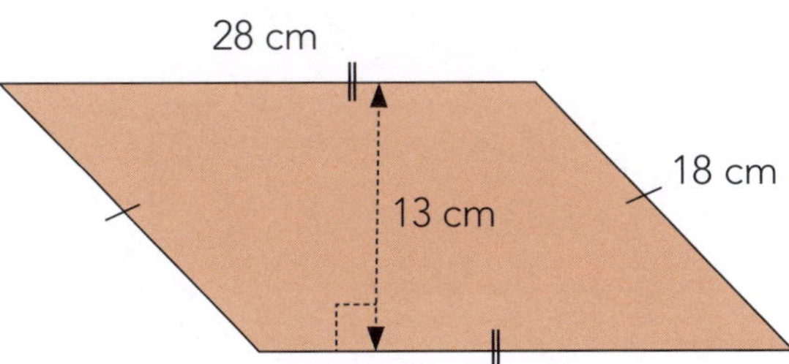

ISBN: 9780170450454

7

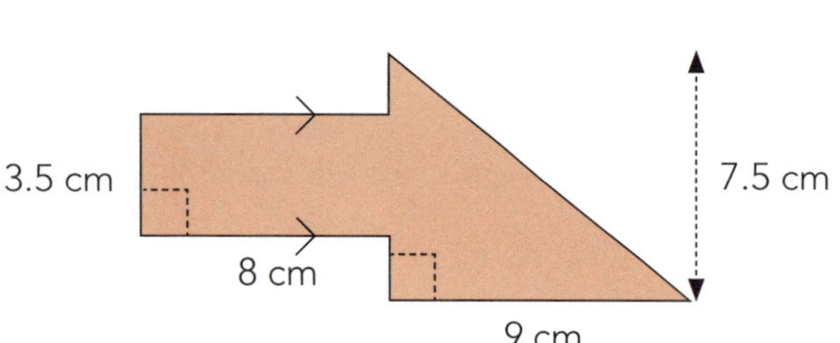

8

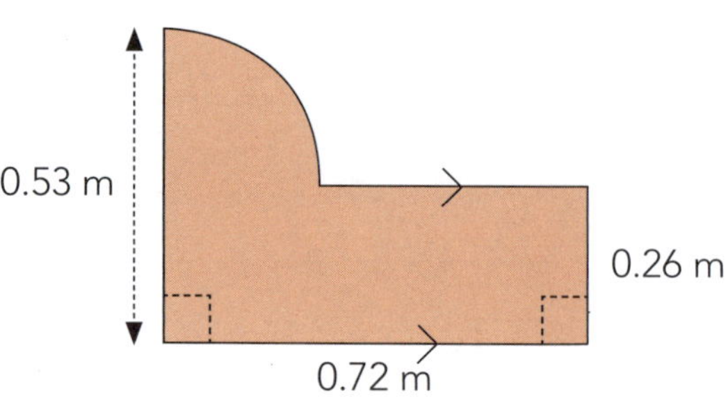

9

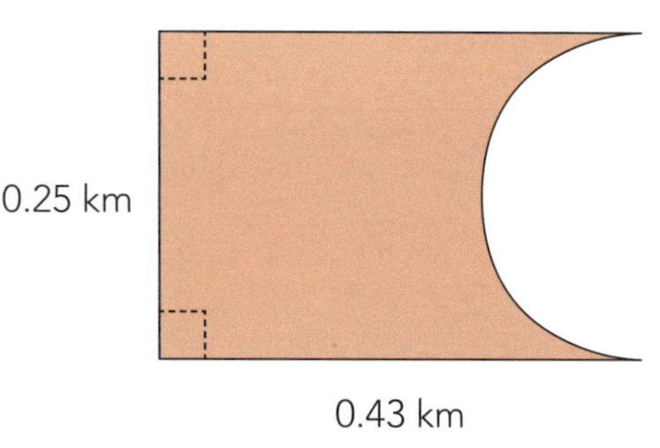

10 Rectangles have been removed from a triangle.

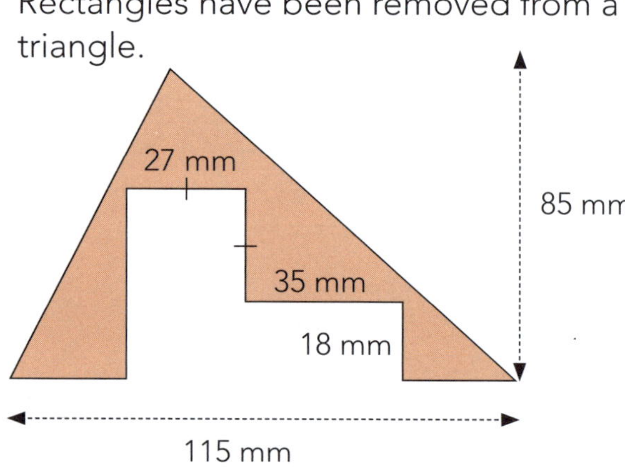

11

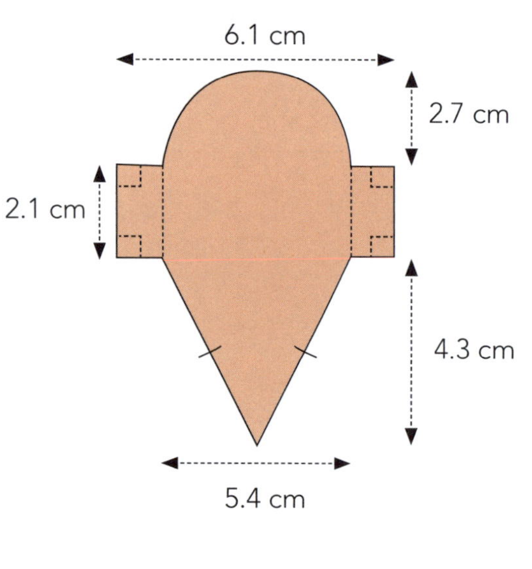

12

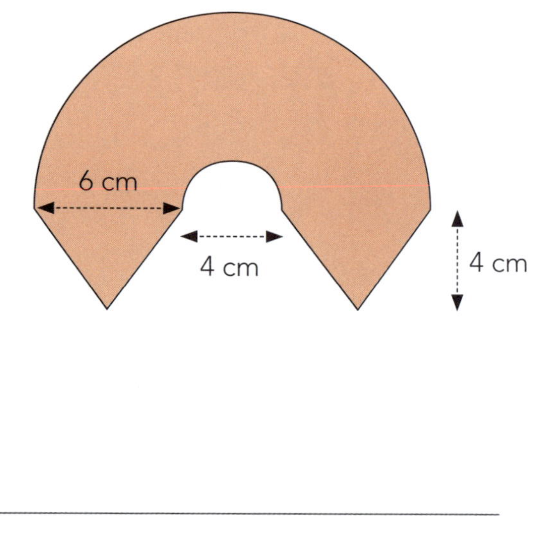

 ISBN: 9780170450454

Word questions

Answer the following questions. Don't forget to sketch a diagram first.

1 Edward's square paddock (sides 45.3m) contains a rectangular water trough that is 1.6 m by 80 cm. What area is available for his horse to graze?

2 A circular pool (diameter 4.3 m) has a strip of tiles around it. Each tile is 6.5 cm high. Calculate the area of tiling.

3 A square wedding cake (30 cm per side) needs to sit on a square base that is big enough for a 4 cm edge on all four sides. Calculate the area of the base.

4 What would be the area of a circular base for a circular cake (diameter 30 cm) if it had a 4 cm edge around it?

5 A regular half-hexagon has short sides of 12 cm, a long side that is double that, and a vertical height of 10.4 cm. Calculate its area.

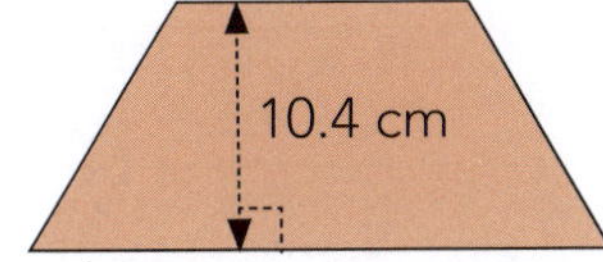

6 A rabbit enclosure (2.7 m by 1.8 m) contains a hutch that is rectangular and 85 cm by 35 cm. Calculate the area of the enclosure that is not taken up by hutch.

7 **a** Maggie's lawn is rectangular and 23 m wide and 28.5 m long. In the centre is a circular herb garden, which has a diameter of 3.5 m. Calculate the area of lawn.

b Fertiliser is to be applied to the lawn at a rate of 15 g per square metre. Fertiliser comes in 8 kg bags. How many bags of fertiliser will Maggie need to buy, and how much will be left over?

8 **a** Brian needs to paint two sides, two ends and the top of a block wall. It is 7.3 m long, 1.6 m high and 20 cm deep. Calculate the area that needs to be painted.

b The paint covers 11 m^2 per litre, and he needs to apply two coats of paint. The paint is sold in only 1 L or 3 L cans. How many litres of paint will he need to buy, and how much will be left over?

9 **a** A cake is made in a ring tin, so it has a circular hole in the middle. If the diameter of the tin is 21 cm and the hole has a diameter of 50 mm, calculate the area of the icing on the top of the cake.

b The cake is 7 cm deep. Calculate the total area of icing if the sides (including inside the hole) are iced as well.

ISBN: 9780170450454

Challenge 3

Calculate the percentage of area that is shaded area in each of these drawings. Each is constructed using only semicircles or quarter circles with a diameter or radius of 10 cm.

1 **a**

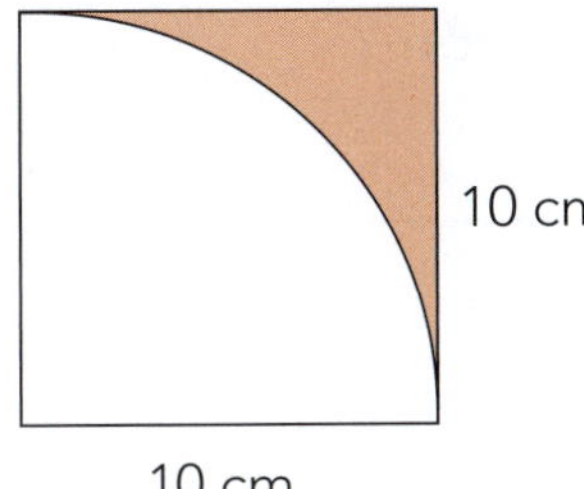

b

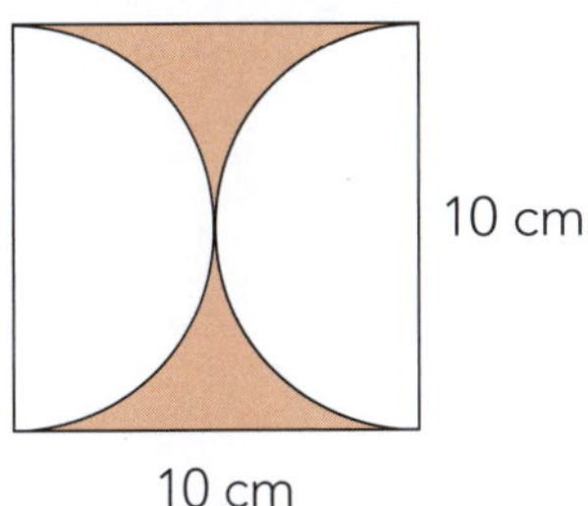

c What do you notice about your answers to **a** and **b**?

d

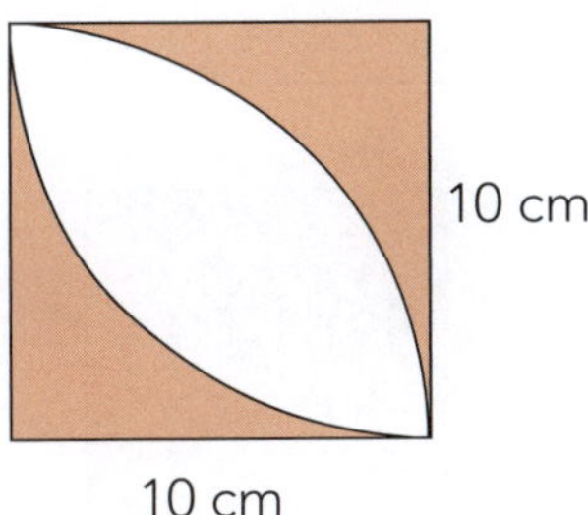

e

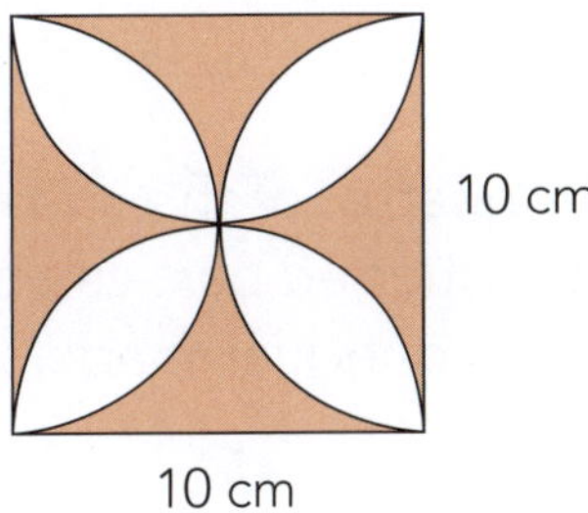

f What do you notice about your answers to **d** and **e**?

Tough nuts

g

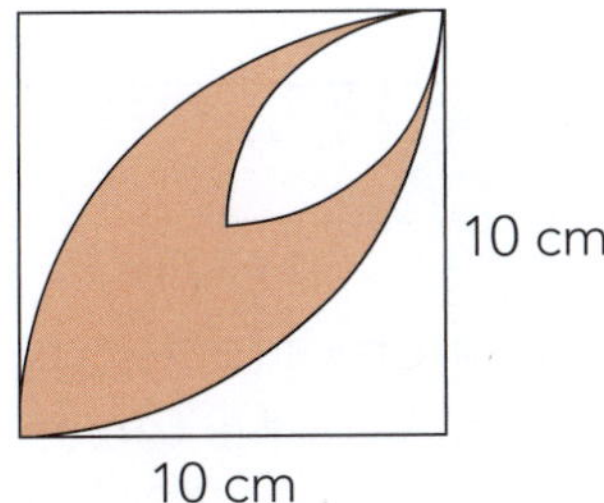

h

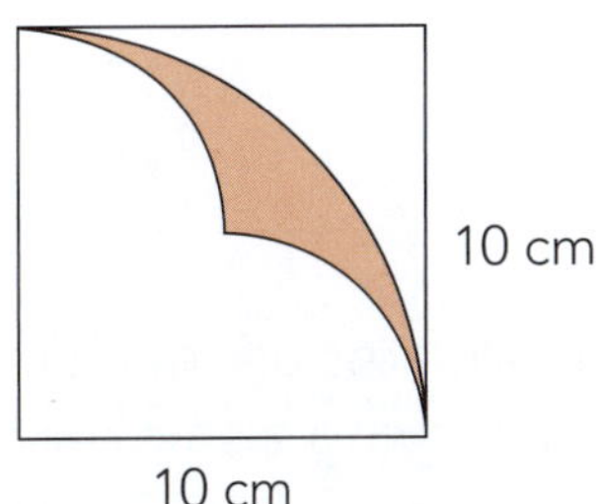

ISBN: 9780170450454

Challenge 4

Answer the following questions.

1 A rectangular room has a perimeter of 30 m. If the lengths of the walls can only be integers, what is the maximum possible area of the room?

2 A garden is twice as long as it is wide. If its area is is 72 m^2, how long is the garden?

3 One quarter of the square is shaded. Show how the unshaded part can be divided into four shapes of equal shape and equal area.

4 Two pizzas cost the same amount. One is an 18 cm square pizza and the other is a round pizza with a diameter of 20 cm. Which is better value? Explain your answer.

5 Two squares are each removed by single straight cuts from a rectangular piece of card, leaving a smaller rectangle which is 2 cm by 3 cm. What is the smallest possible area of the original piece of card?

 ISBN: 9780170450454

Surface area

- The surface area of an object is the **sum** of the areas of **all its faces and surfaces**.

Examples:

1 Find the surface area of a cuboid that is 5 cm high, 10 cm wide and 7.5 cm deep.

Start by drawing a diagram.

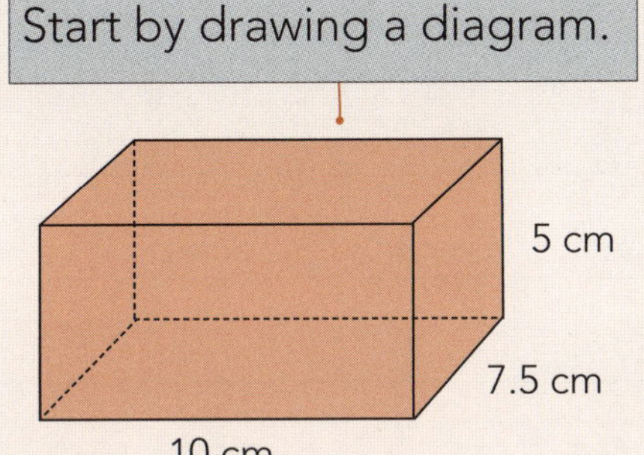

Opposite surfaces have the same area.

Ceiling and floor: Area = 2(10 x 7.5) = 150 cm^2

Front and back walls: Area = 2(10 x 5) = 100 cm^2

Side walls: Area = 2(7.5 x 5) = 75 cm^2

Total surface area: 150 + 100 + 75 = 325 cm^2

2 Find the surface area of a cylinder that is 12 cm high and has a radius of 5 cm.

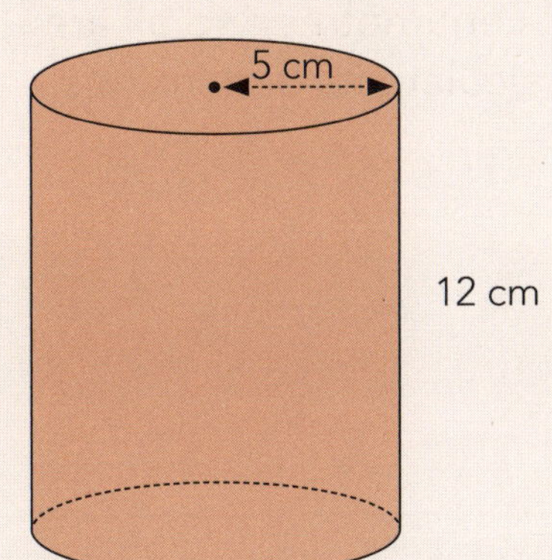

The top and bottom are circles with a radius of 5 cm:

Area = 2(π x 5^2) = 157.08 cm^2 (2 dp)

The sides are a rectangle 12 cm high and a width equal to the circumference of the circle:

Think about cutting the label off a can.

Area = 12 x (πd)

= 12 x (π x 2 x 5)

= 376.99 cm^2 (2 dp)

Total surface area: 157.08 + 376.99 = 534.07 cm^2 (2 dp)

Calculate the surface areas of the following shapes.

1 A cube with 20 cm edges.

2 A cuboid that is 20 cm high, 30 cm wide and 40 cm deep.

ISBN: 9780170450454

3 A cylinder that is 10 cm high and has a radius of 10 cm.

4 A cylinder that is 1 m high and has a radius of 20 cm. Write your answer in square centimetres (cm^2).

Answer the following questions.

5 A cube has a surface area of 384 cm^2. Calculate the length of one edge.

6 A cuboid has a surface area of 142 cm^2. The lengths of its edges are all prime numbers of centimetres and all are different. Calculate its dimensions.

7 This shape is made up of a cube and a cuboid. Calculate its surface area.

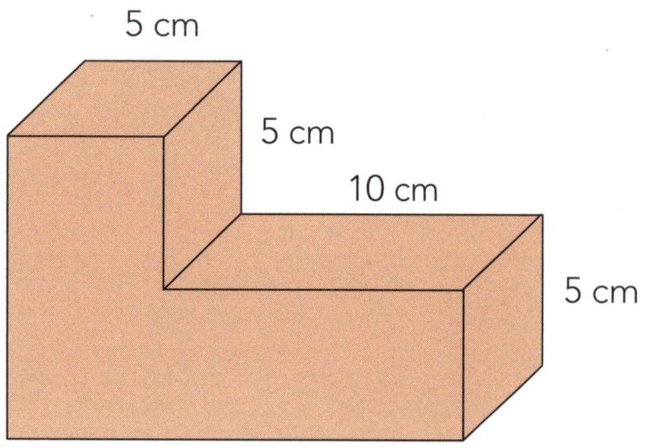

5 cm

5 cm

10 cm

5 cm

ISBN: 9780170450454

Challenge 5

There is at least one mistake in the following calculations. Write the correct working and explain what went wrong.

	Question	Answer	Corrected answer
1	Calculate the shaded area. 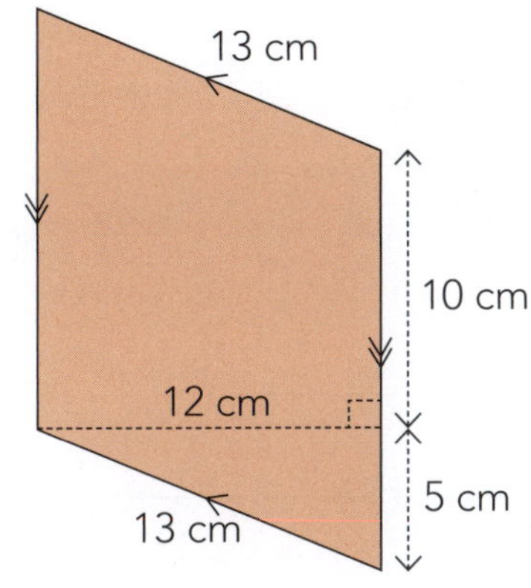	Area = 15 x 13 = 195 cm^2	
	What went wrong:		
2	Calculate the circumference of a circle that has a radius of 7 cm.	Circumference = π x 7^2 = 153.94 cm^2 (2 dp)	
	What went wrong:		
3	Calculate the shaded area. 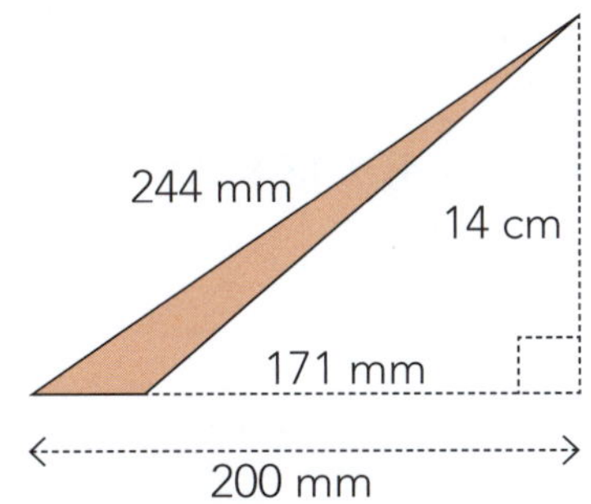	Area = $\frac{1}{2}$ x 171 x 14 = 1197 mm^2	
	What went wrong:		
4	Calculate the area of a semicircle that has a diameter of 18 cm.	Area = $\frac{1}{2}$ x π x 18^2 = 508.94 cm^2	
	What went wrong:		

ISBN: 9780170450454

	Question	Answer	Corrected answer
5	The surface area of a cube is 8.64 m^2. Calculate the length of one edge.	Area of one face $= \dfrac{8.64}{6}$ $= 1.44\ \text{m}^2$ So edge length $= \dfrac{1.44}{4}$ $= 0.36\ \text{m}$	

What went wrong:

6 Calculate the perimeter of this shape.

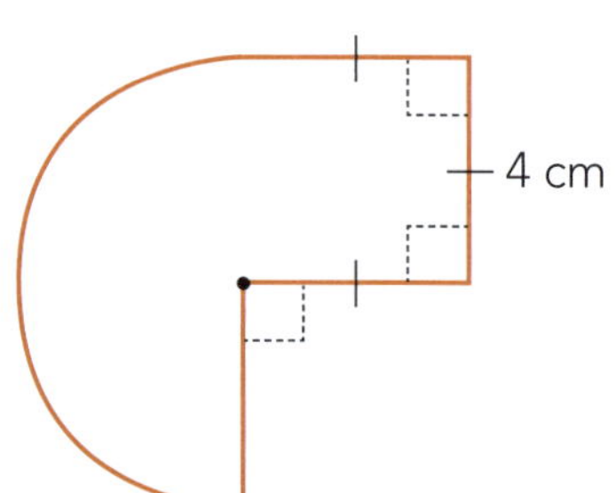

Perimeter $= (3 \times 4) + \left(\dfrac{1}{2} \times \pi \times 8\right)$

$= 24.57$ cm (2 dp)

What went wrong:

7 Calculate the surface area of a cylinder that has a height of 2.1 m and a diameter of 150 cm.

SA $= (\pi \times\ 0.75^2) + (2\pi \times 0.75 \times 2.1)$

$= 11.66\ \text{m}^2$ (2 dp)

What went wrong:

8 Kerry needs to paint the entire surface area of five planks of wood. Each plank is 4 m long, 12 cm wide and 5 cm deep. Calculate the total surface area of the five planks.

SA $= 5[(2 \times 0.12 \times 4) + (2 \times 0.5 \times 4) + (2 \times 0.5 \times 0.12)]$

$= 5[5.08]$

$= 25.4\ \text{m}^2$

What went wrong:

 ISBN: 9780170450454

Volume

Units of volume

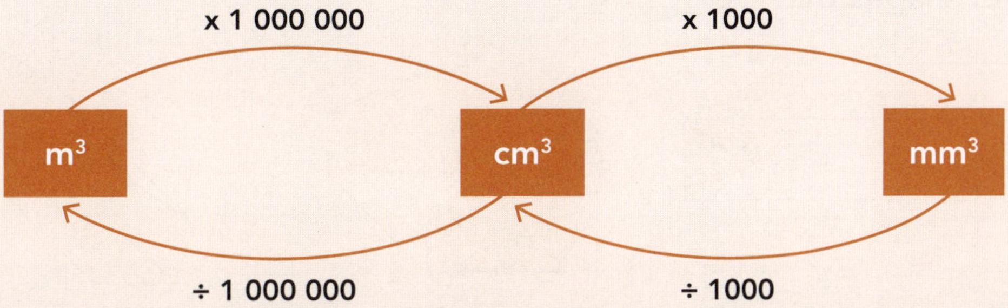

x 1 000 000 : m³ → cm³ ; x 1000 : cm³ → mm³

÷ 1 000 000 : cm³ → m³ ; ÷ 1000 : mm³ → cm³

Reminder: Relationship between volume (m³, cm³, mm³) and capacity (L, mL):

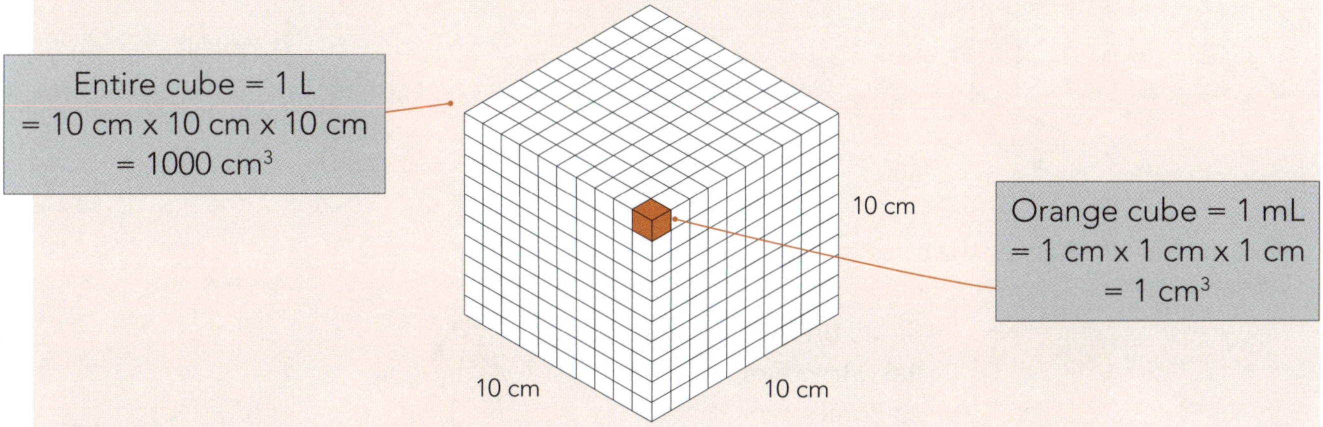

Entire cube = 1 L
= 10 cm x 10 cm x 10 cm
= 1000 cm³

Orange cube = 1 mL
= 1 cm x 1 cm x 1 cm
= 1 cm³

10 cm, 10 cm, 10 cm

Also: 1 m³ = 100 cm x 100 cm x 100 cm
= 1000 L

Highlight the correct conversion for each of the following.

1	5000 cm³	500 000 mm³	0.005 m³
		0.05 m³	50 000 mm³
2	9000 cm³	0.09 m³	90 000 m³
		900 000 mm³	0.009 m³
3	600 000 mm³	0.006 m³	60 cm³
		0.0006 m³	6000 cm³
4	7.2 m³	7200 cm³	7 200 000 cm³
		72 000 cm³	720 000 cm³
5	0.0011 m³	110 cm³	110 000 mm³
		1100 cm³	11 000 mm³
6	0.099 m³	99 000 cm³	9 900 000 mm³
		9900 cm³	990 000 cm³

ISBN: 9780170450454

Prisms

- A **prism** is a shape that has **two identical parallel faces** and **flat sides**.

Volume of a prism = area of face x depth

Examples of shapes that are prisms:

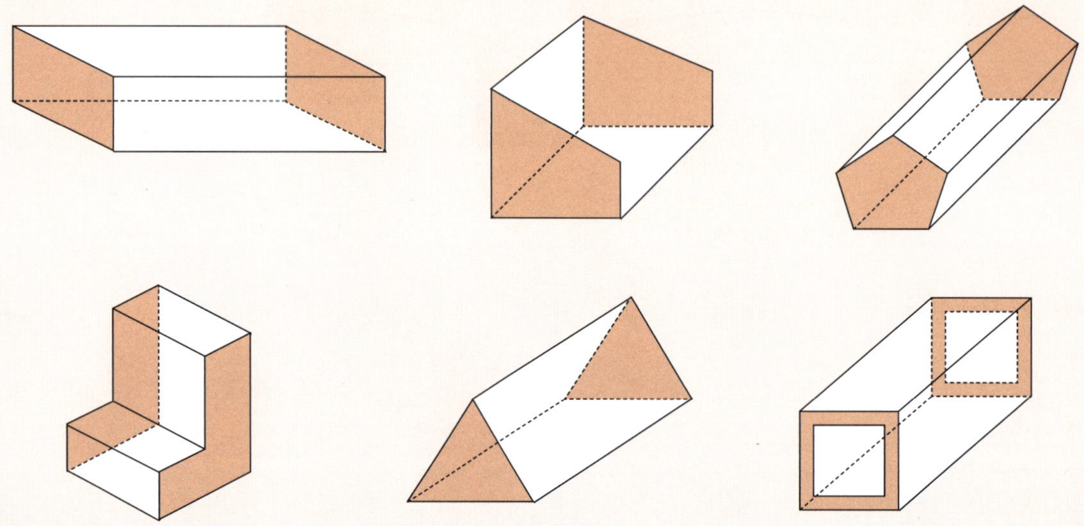

Examples of shapes that are not prisms:

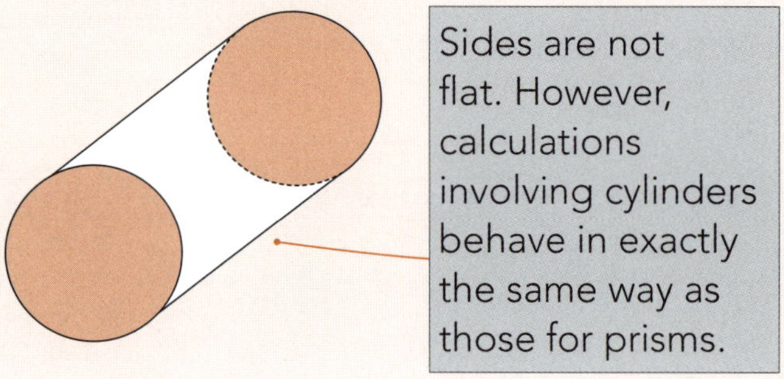

Sides are not flat. However, calculations involving cylinders behave in exactly the same way as those for prisms.

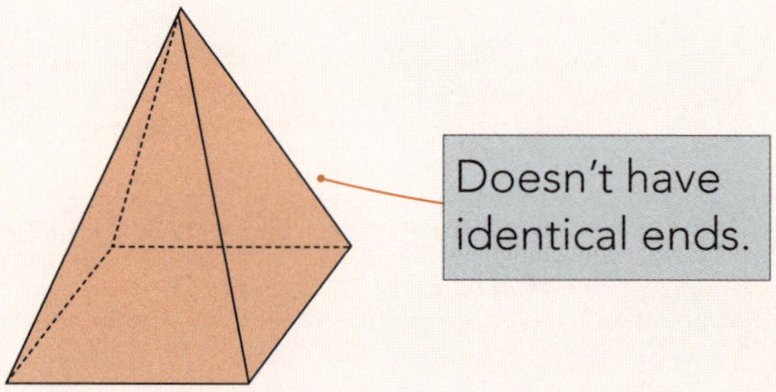

Doesn't have identical ends.

Which of the following figures are prisms? (✓ or ×).

1 ☐

2 ☐

3 ☐

4 ☐

5 ☐

6 ☐

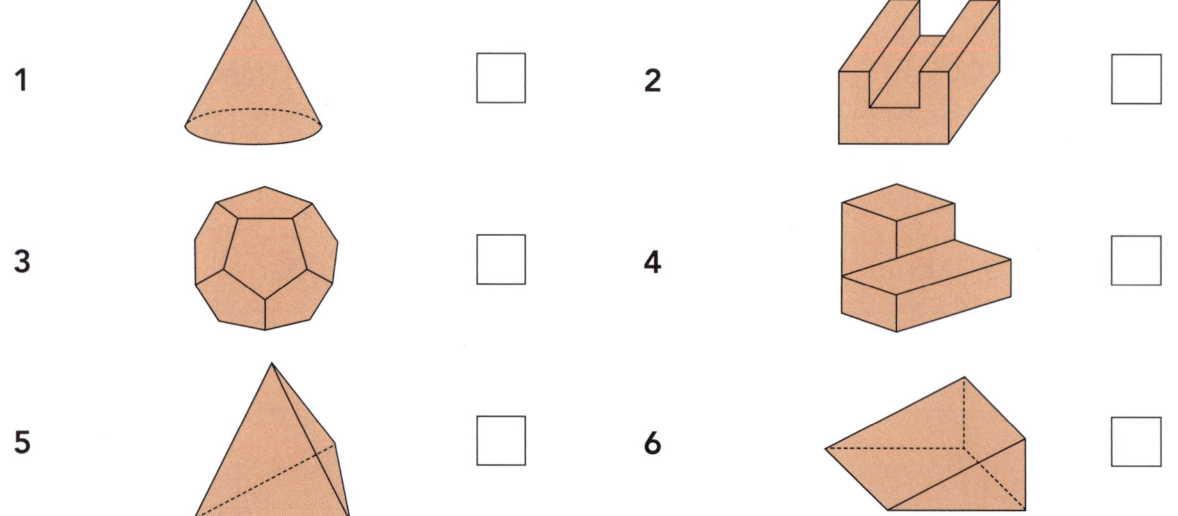

ISBN: 9780170450454

Cuboids

- The volume of a three-dimensional (3D) shape is the amount of **space** the shape occupies.
- A **cuboid** is a box shape, e.g. a shoebox.
- A **cube** is a box shape where all the dimensions are equal, e.g. a die.

If you can **fill** it, it's volume.

Volume = height x width x depth

$V = h \times w \times d$

Examples:

1

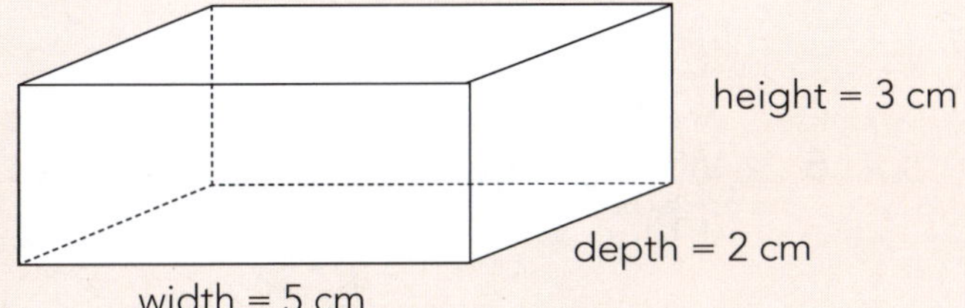

Volume = $h \times w \times d$
= $3 \times 5 \times 2$
= 30 cm^3

2 Another way to think about it is to find the area of the 'face' and multiply it by the depth.

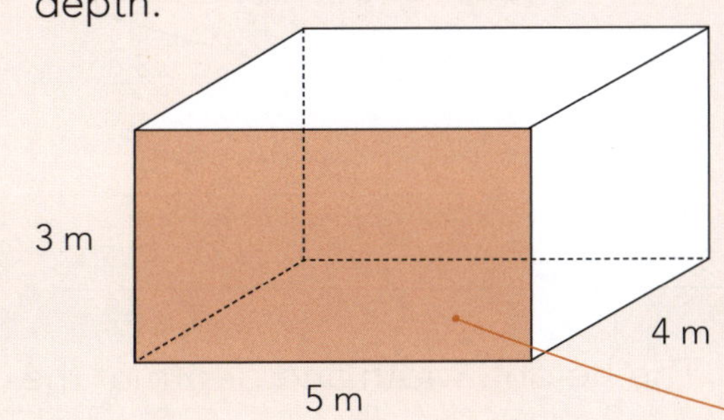

Volume = **area of face** x d
= **(3 x 5)** x 4
= **(15)** x 4
= 60 m^3

Area of the face is **15 m^2**, which is multiplied by the depth (4 m).

Calculate the volumes of these cuboids.

1

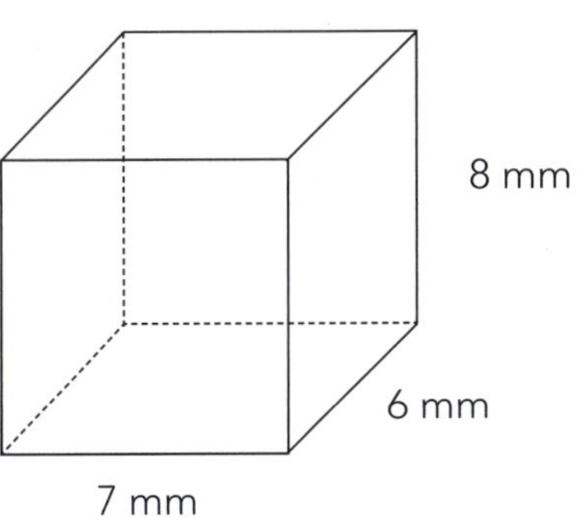

____

____

2

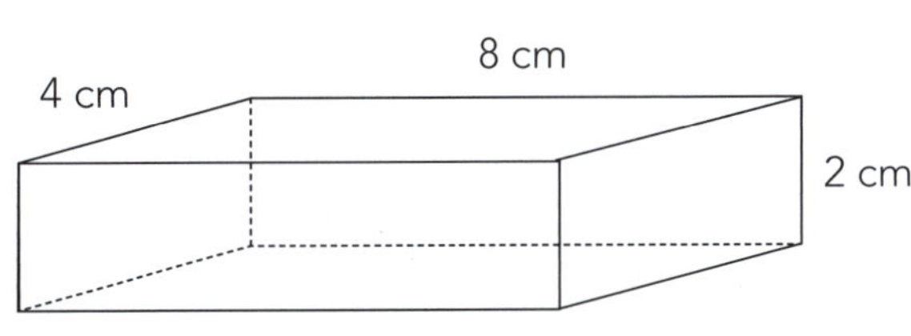

____

____

ISBN: 9780170450454

3

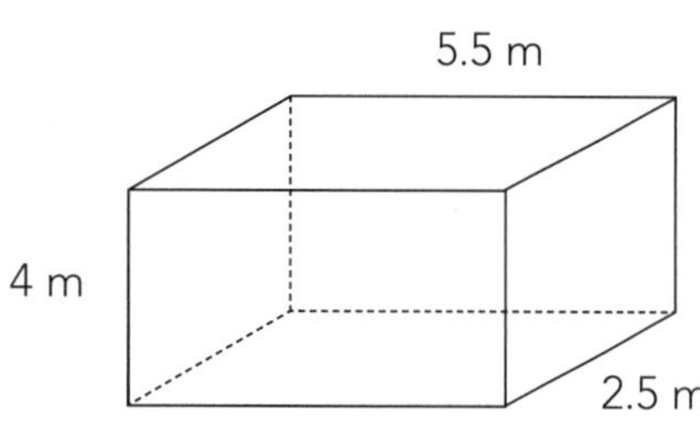

4

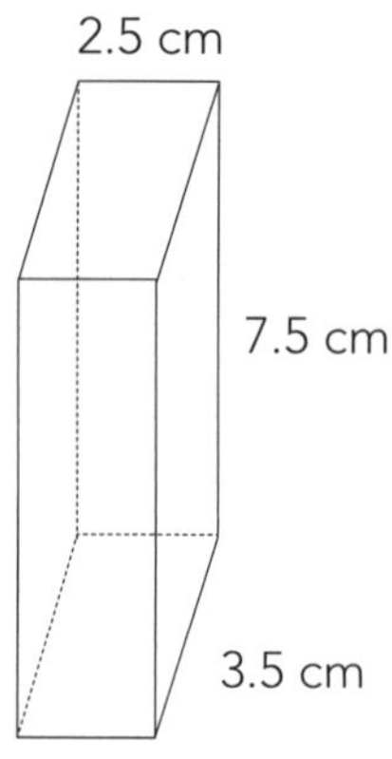

5 Write your answer in cubic centimetres (cm^3).

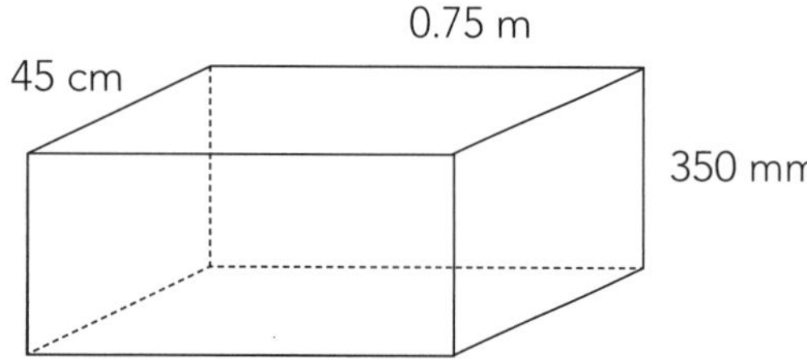

6 Write your answer in cubic metres (m^3).

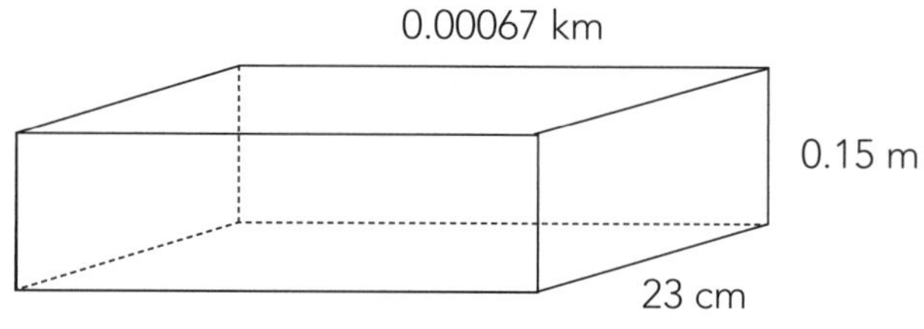

7 This cube and cuboid have the same volume. The height, width and depth of the cuboid are different whole numbers. Write the dimensions on the diagram.

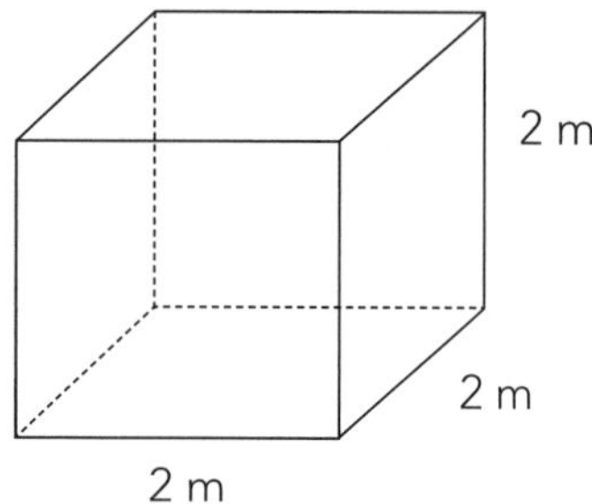

8 The volume of a cuboid is 648 cm^3. It has two dimensions of 6 cm and 90 mm. What is the third dimension of the cuboid?

9 A rectangular crate measures 120 cm by 100 cm by 80 cm. Boxes are to be stacked inside this crate. They measure 6 cm by 8 cm by 4 cm. How many boxes will fit inside the crate?

ISBN: 9780170450454

Compound cuboids

- Some compound cuboids are **prisms**.

Example:

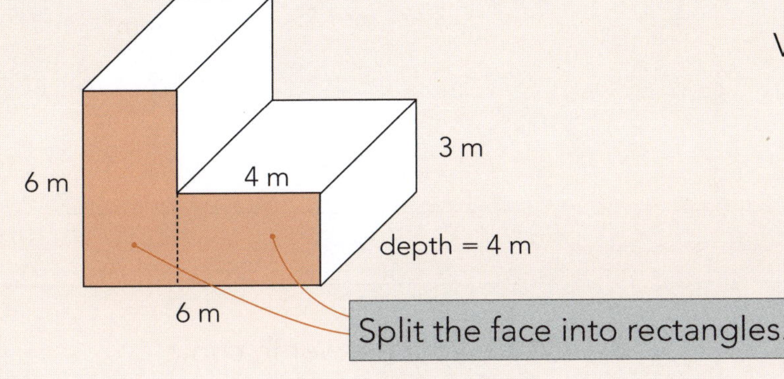

Volume = **area of face** x d

= **((2 x 6) + (4 x 3))** x d

= **(12 + 12)** x d

= **(24)** x 4

= 96 m^3

Calculate the volumes of these compound cuboids.

1

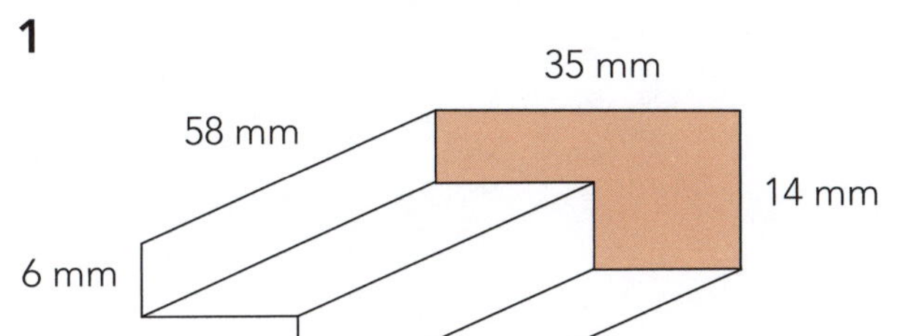

2

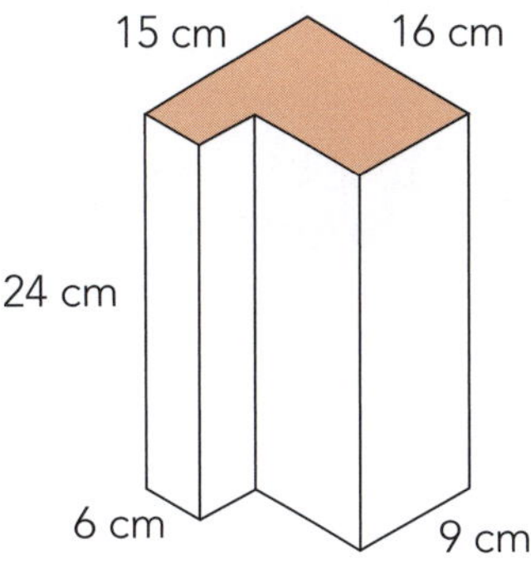

3

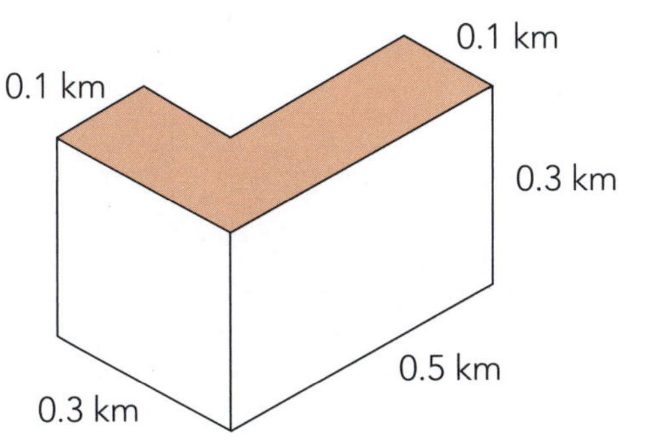

4

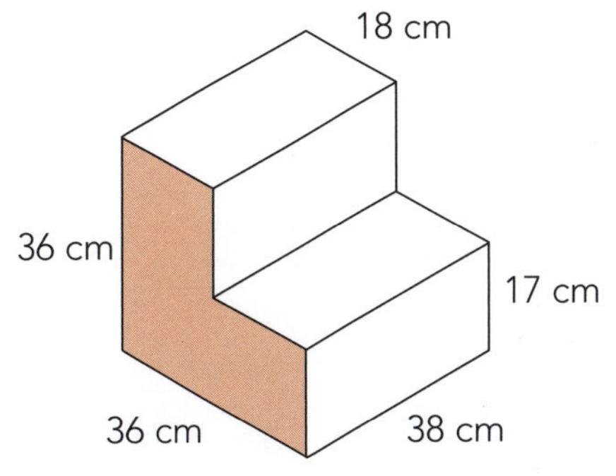

ISBN: 9780170450454

5

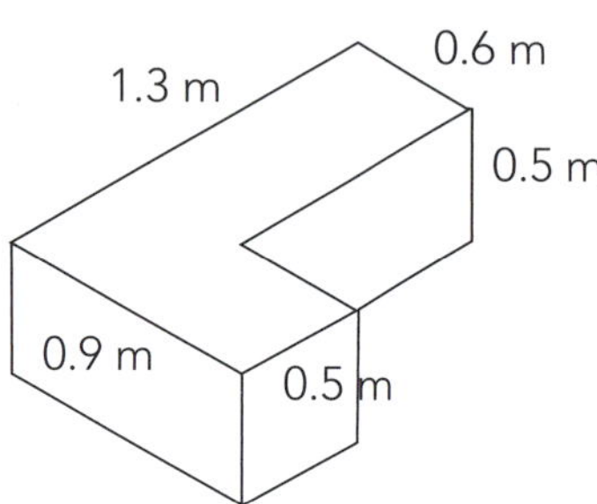

6

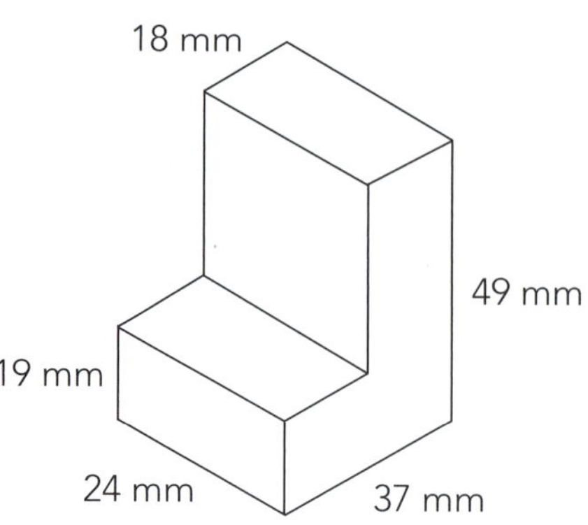

7 Write your answer in cubic centimetres (cm³).

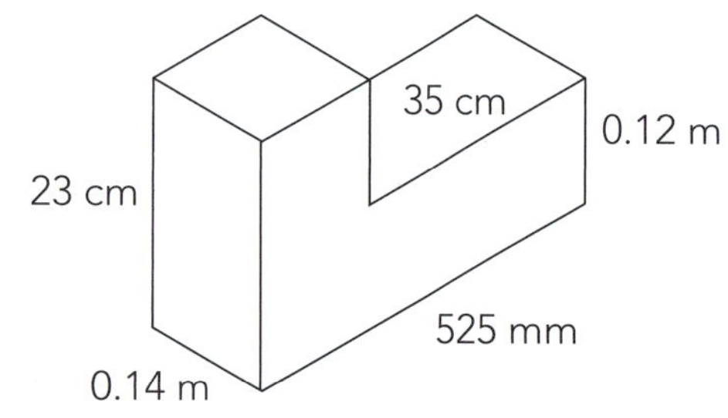

8 Write your answer in cubic centimetres (cm³).

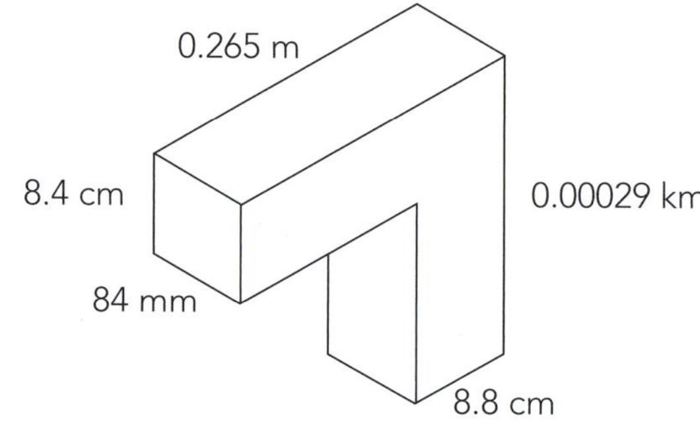

9

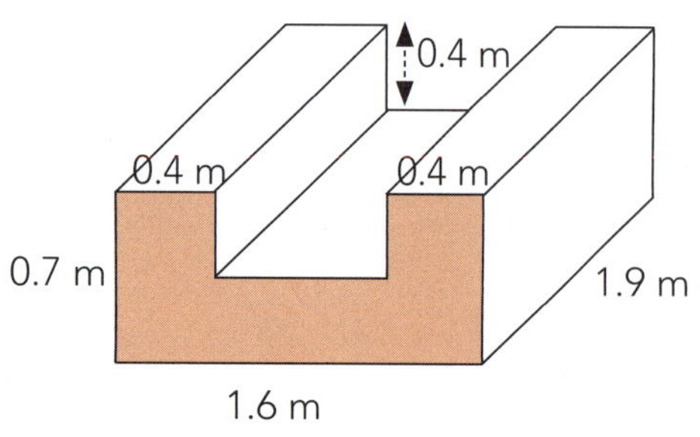

10

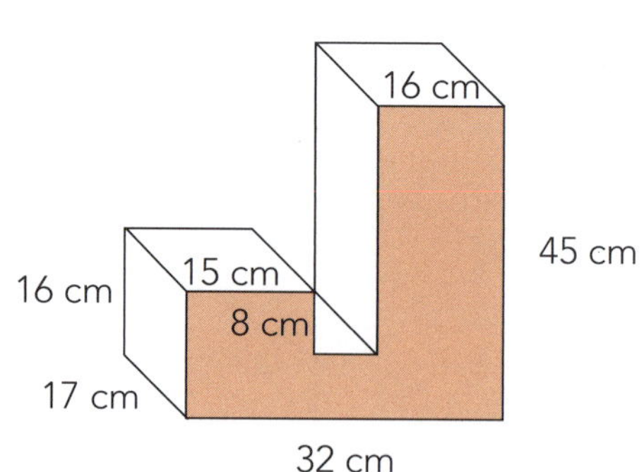

ISBN: 9780170450454

Triangular prisms

- The volume of a triangular prism can be found by finding the area of a face and multiplying by the depth (or length or height).

Volume = area of face x depth

$$= \frac{1}{2} \times \text{base} \times \text{height} \times \text{depth}$$

Examples:

1

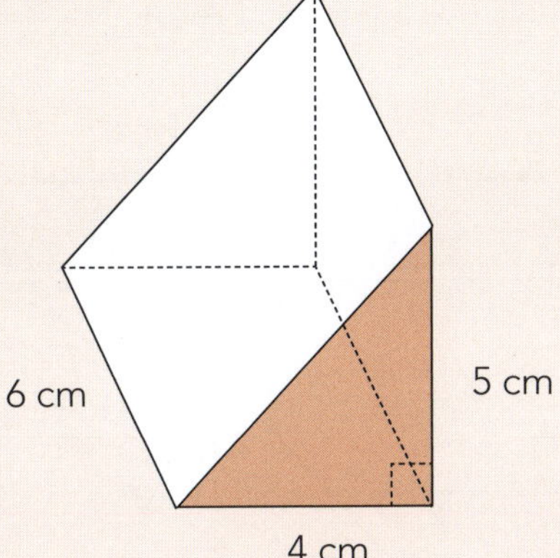

Volume = **area of triangle** x depth

$= \frac{1}{2} \times b \times h \times d$

$= \frac{1}{2} \times 4 \times 5 \times 6$

$= 10\text{ cm}^2 \times 6$

$= 60\text{ cm}^3$

Area of the triangle.

2 Prisms can also be vertical, so find the area of a face and multiply by the height.

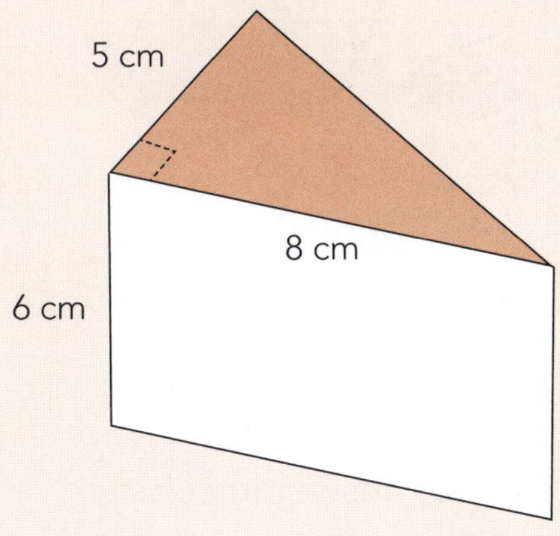

Volume = **area of face** x height

$= \frac{1}{2} \times b \times h \times d$

$= \frac{1}{2} \times 5 \times 8 \times 6$

$= 20\text{ cm}^2 \times 6$

$= 120\text{ cm}^3$

Area of the triangle.

Calculate the volumes of these triangular prisms.

1

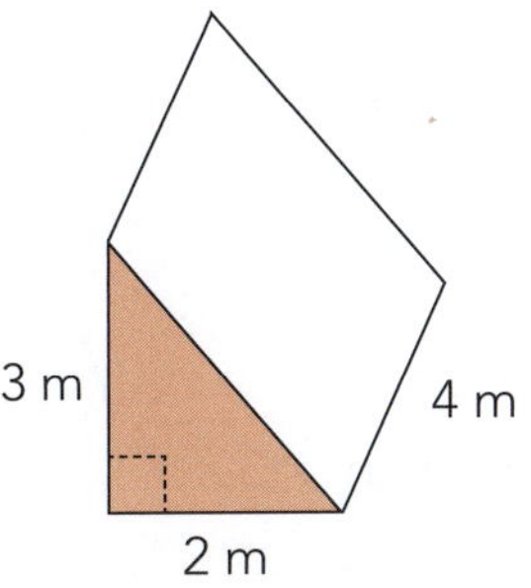

____

____

2

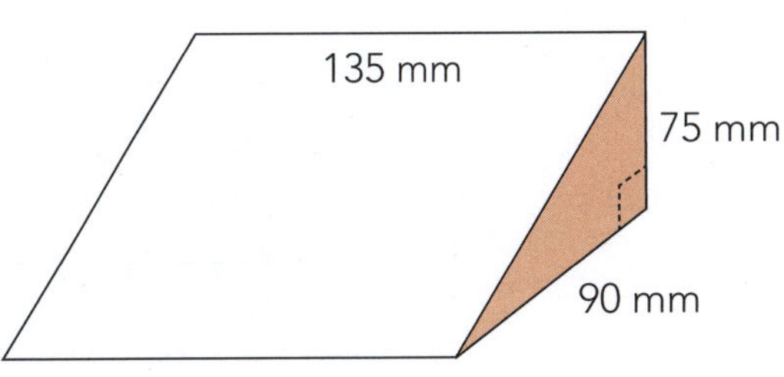

____

____

ISBN: 9780170450454

3

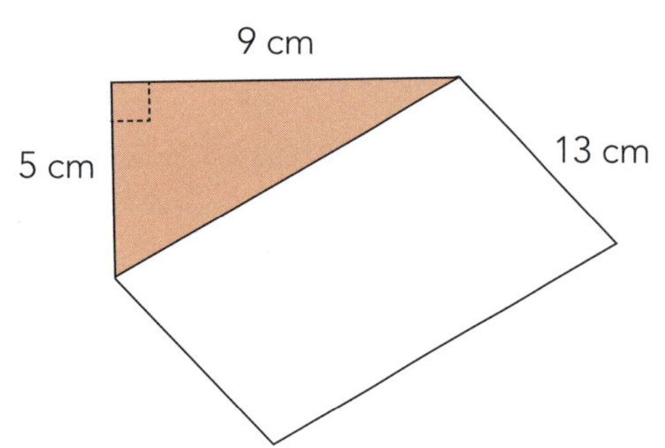

4

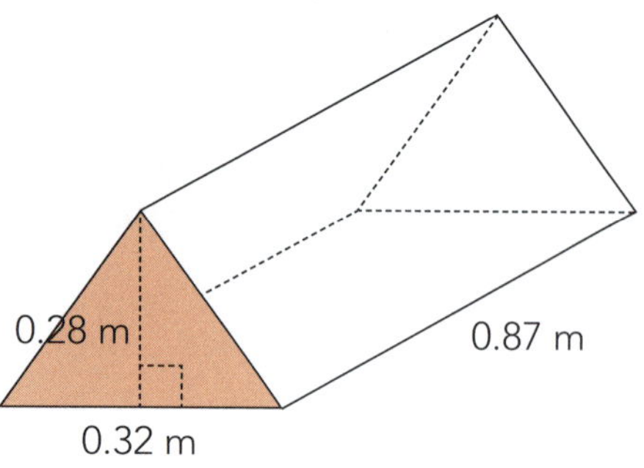

5

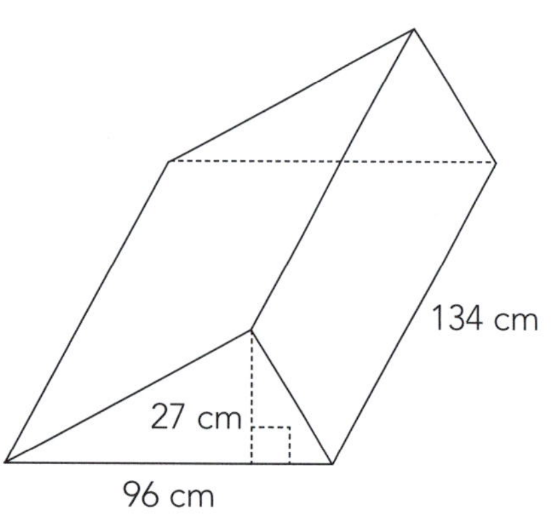

6

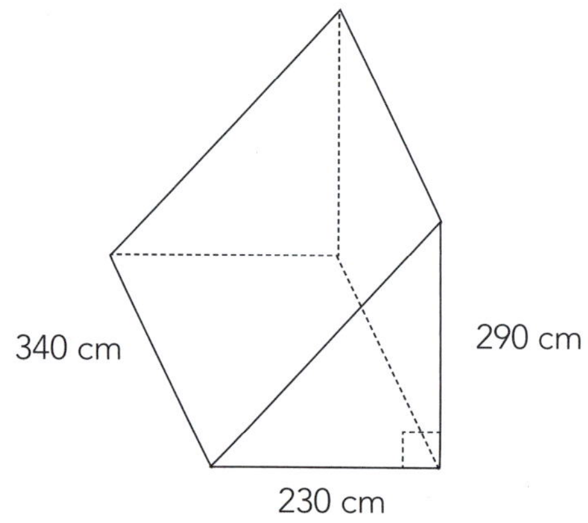

7 Write your answer in cubic metres (m^3).

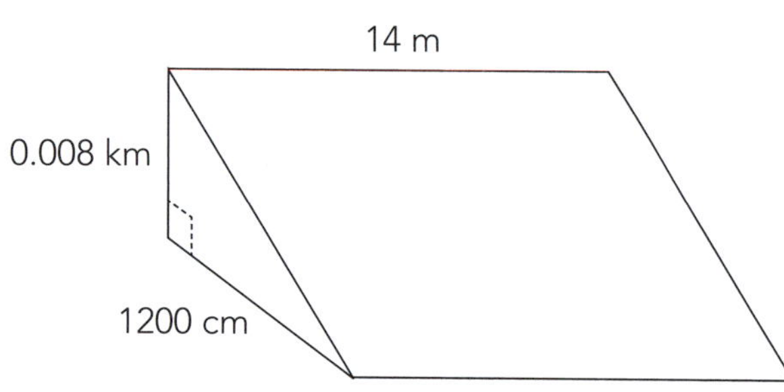

8 Write your answer in cubic centimetres (cm^3).

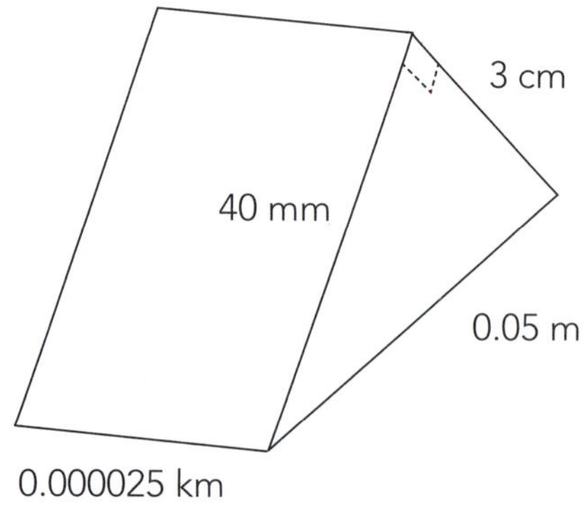

 ISBN: 9780170450454

Other prisms

- The volume of any prism can be found by finding the area of a face and multiplying by the depth (or length or height).

Volume = area of face x depth

Examples:

1

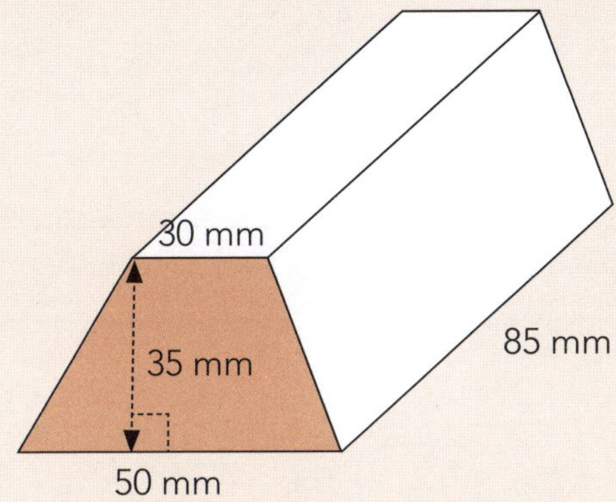

Volume = **area of trapezium** x depth

$= \frac{30 + 50}{2} \times 35 \times 85$

$= 1400 \text{ mm}^2 \times 85$

$= 119\,000 \text{ mm}^3$

2

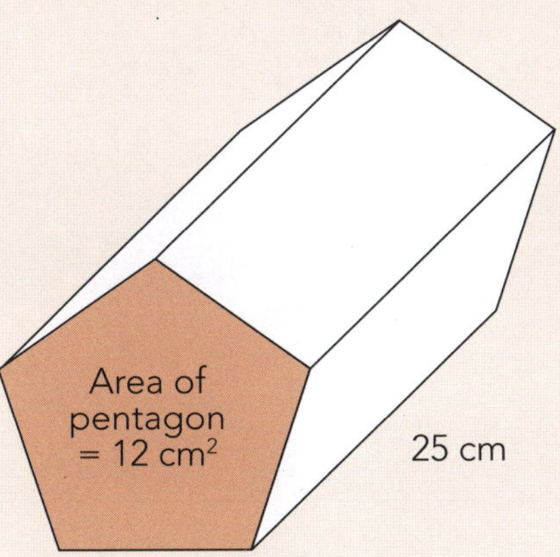

Volume = **area of face** x depth

$= 12 \text{ cm}^2 \times 25$

$= 300 \text{ cm}^3$

Calculate the volumes of these prisms.

1

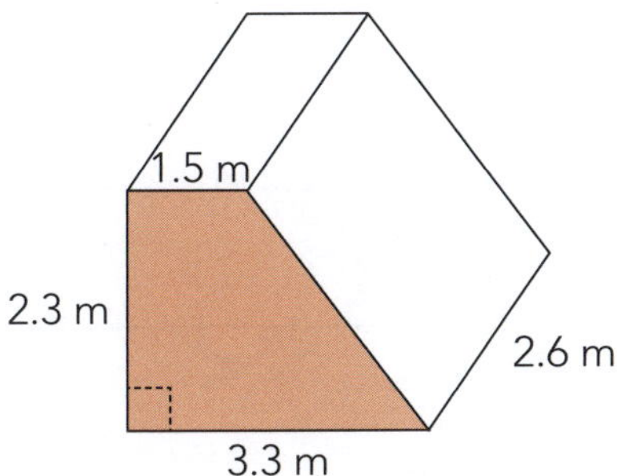

____

____

2

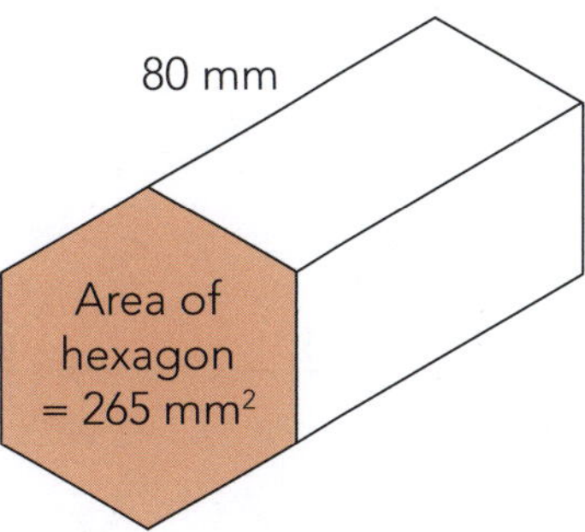

____

____

ISBN: 9780170450454

3

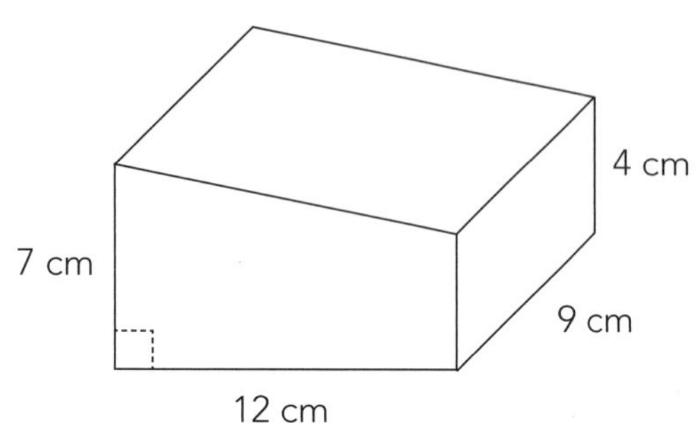

4

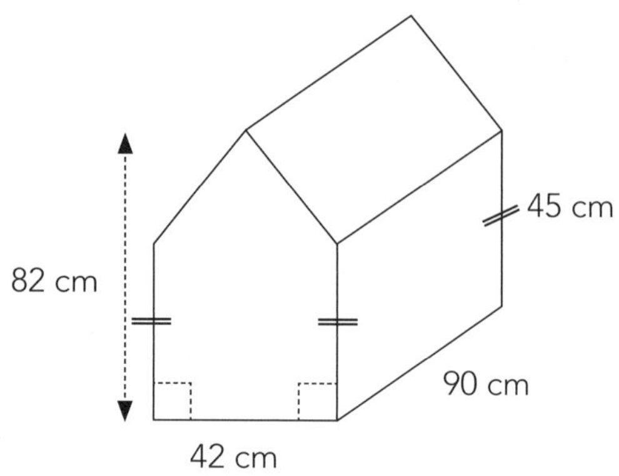

5

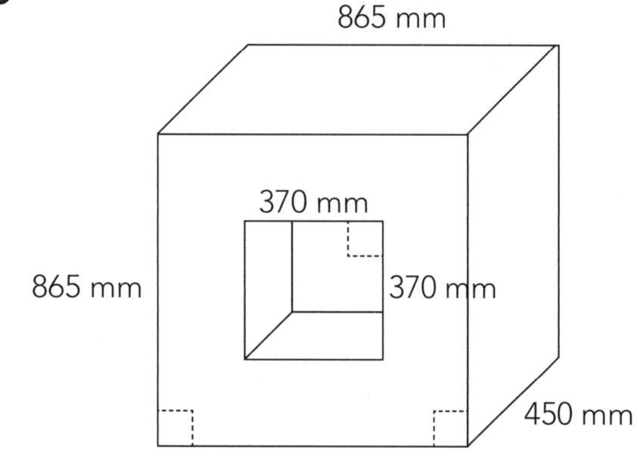

6

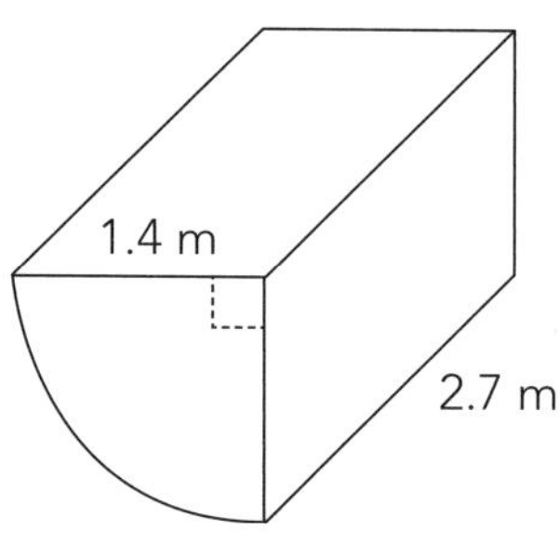

7

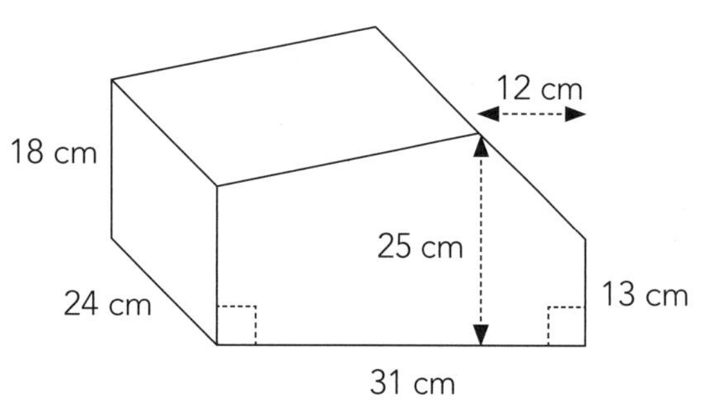

8

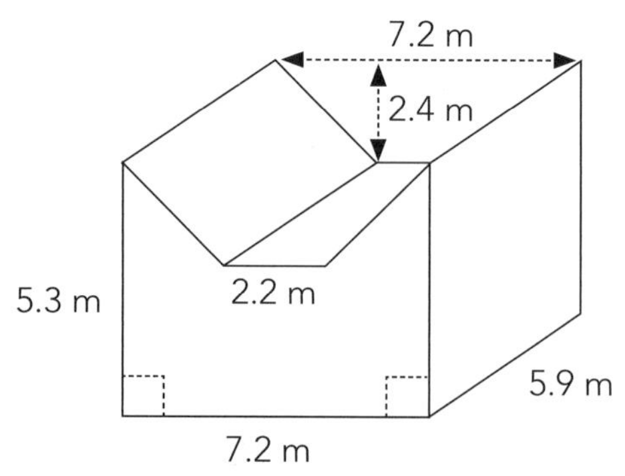

 ISBN: 9780170450454

Cylinders

- The volume of a cylinder can be found by finding the area of a face and multiplying by the depth (or length or height).

Volume = area of face x depth
V = πr^2 x depth

Depth can be replaced by **length** or **height**, depending on the orientation of the cylinder.

Examples:

1

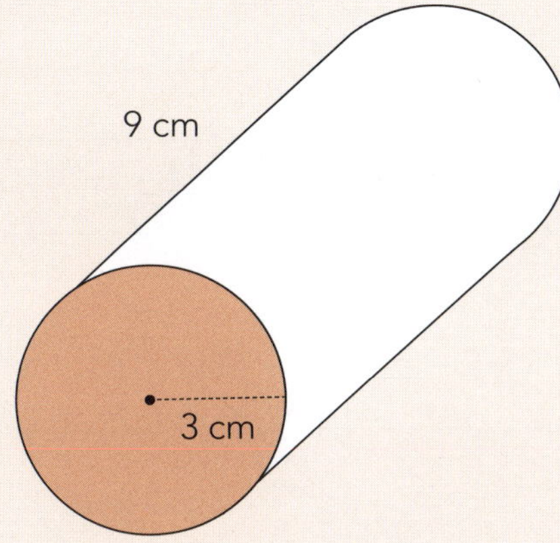

Volume = **area of circle** x length

= $\pi r^2 \times l$

= $\pi \times 3^2 \times 9$

= **28.27 cm²** x 9

= 254.47 cm^3 (2 dp)

Remember to round appropriately.

2 Cylinders can also be vertical, so find the area of a face and multiply by the height.

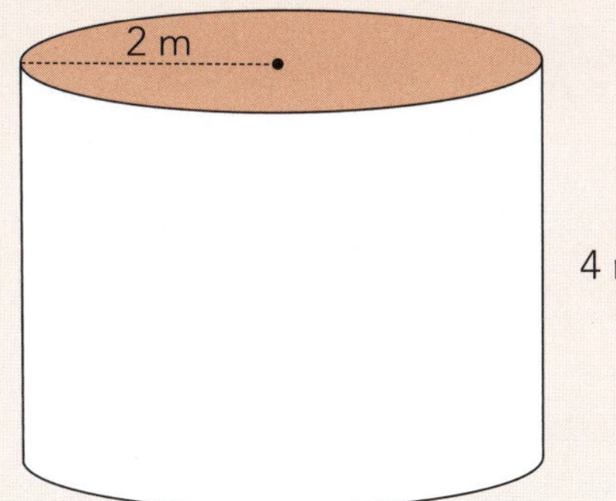

Volume = **area of circle** x height

= $\pi r^2 \times h$

= $\pi \times 2^2 \times 4$

= **12.57 cm²** x 4

= 50.27 m^3 (2 dp)

Calculate the volumes of these cylinders.

1

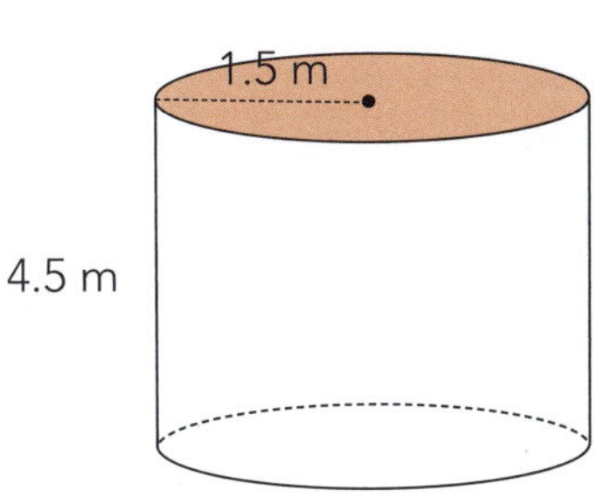

____

____

2

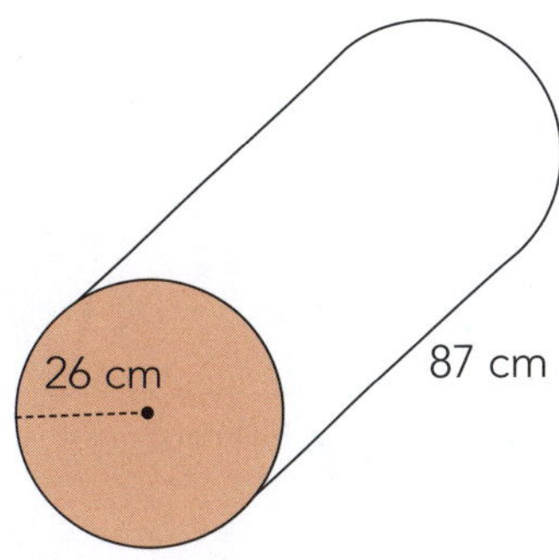

____

____

ISBN: 9780170450454

3

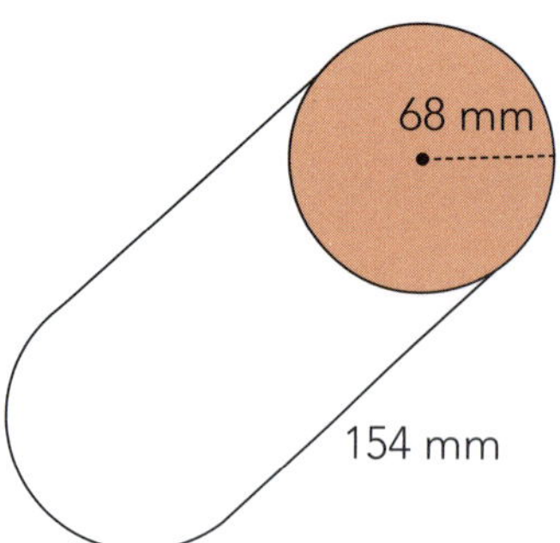

4

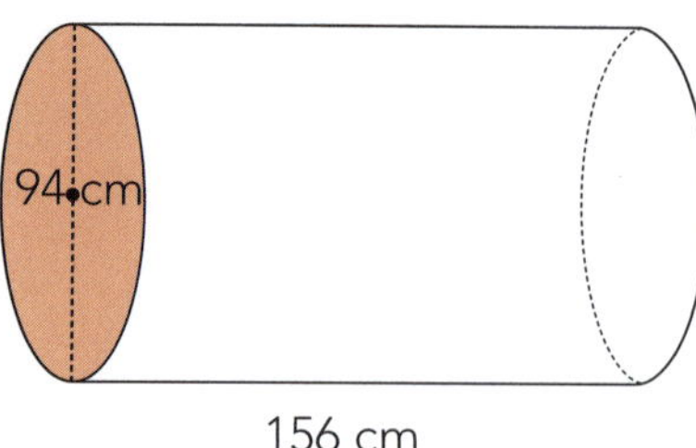

5

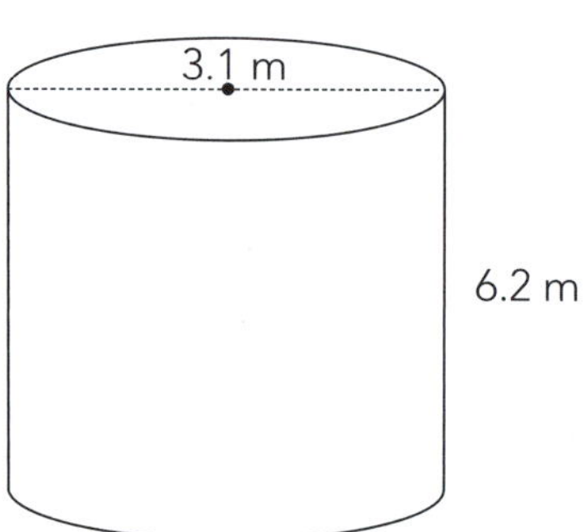

6

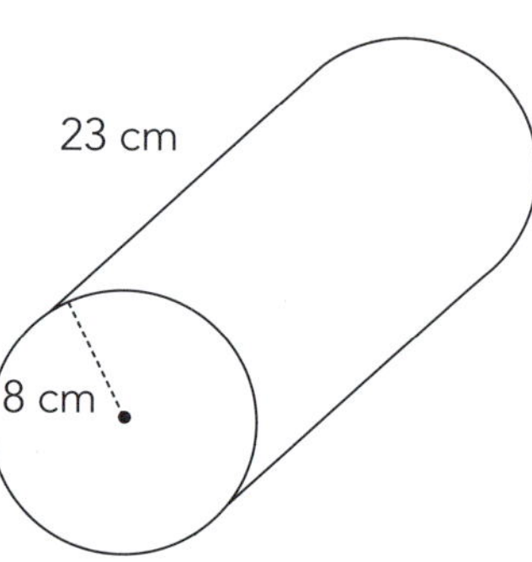

7 Write your answer in cubic centimetres (cm^3).

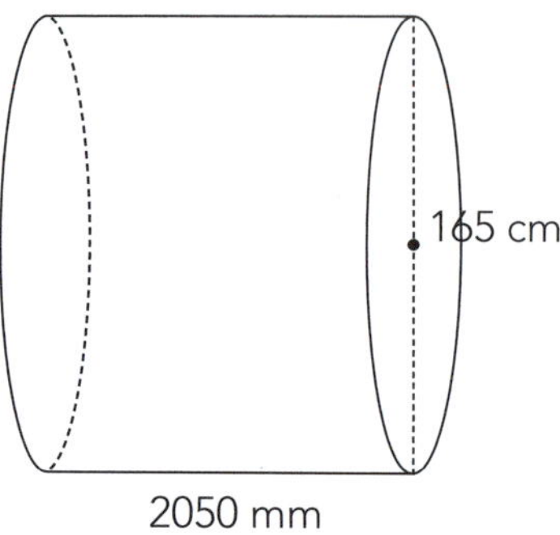

8 Write your answer in cubic centimetres (cm^3).

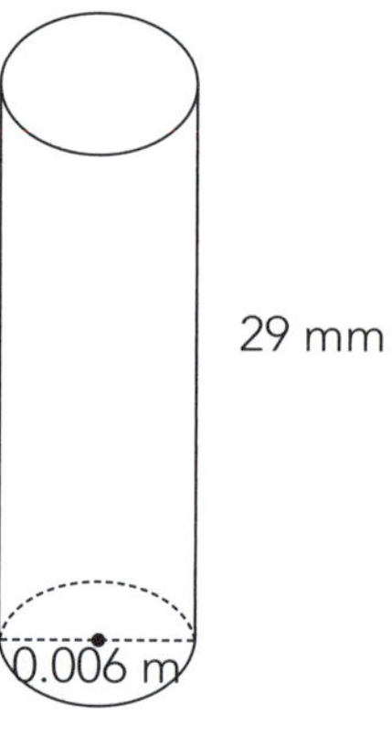

 ISBN: 9780170450454

Word questions

1 A cube has a depth of 15 cm. What is the volume of the cube?

2 A cylinder has a diameter of 0.5 m and a height of 3.5 m. Calculate its volume.

3 A triangular prism has a vertical height of 90 mm, a base of 120 mm and a length of 150 mm. What is the volume of this prism?

4 The vertical height, base and length of a triangular prism are all prime numbers. Its volume is 82.5 cm^3. What values can the three dimensions take?

5 A cuboid has a height twice its width and has a depth of 10 cm. If the volume of the cuboid is 720 cm^3, calculate the height and the width of the cuboid.

6 A piece of A4 is 21 cm wide, 29.7 cm high and 0.05 mm thick. Calculate its volume in mm^3 and in cm^3.

7 How many 2.25 L bottles of soft drink would you need to buy in order to completely fill a tank that has an internal volume of one cubic metre?

8 A cylindrical glass has the following external dimensions: radius 4 cm, height 12 cm. If the walls and floor of the glass are both 3 mm thick, what volume of molten glass was needed to make it?

ISBN: 9780170450454

9 **a** A carton contains 2 litres of orange juice. How many cylindrical glasses with an internal height of 10 cm and an internal radius of 3 cm can be filled from the carton? Remember, 1 L = 1000 cm^3.

b If you have to leave a 1 cm gap at the top of the glass so there are no spillages, does this change your answer?

10 Lucy needs a container to hold 650 cm^3. Which of these shapes do you suggest she selects? Why?

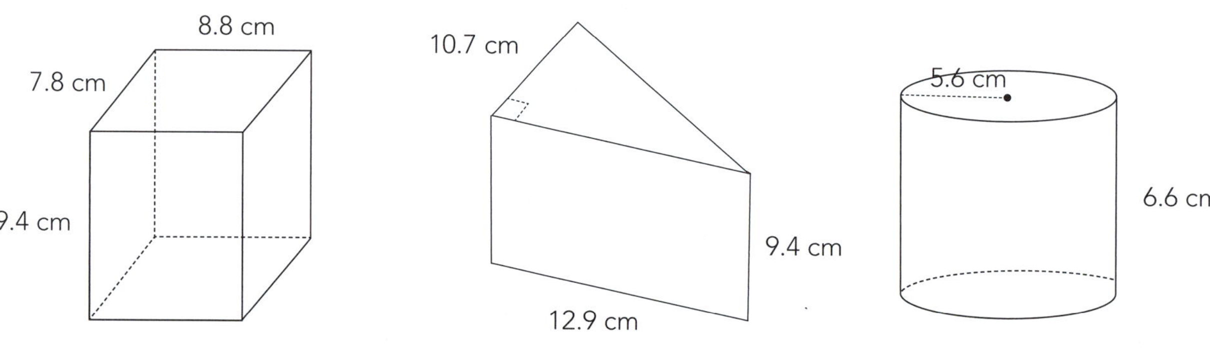

11 Consider a solid cylinder that fits exactly inside a cube. The length of one edge of the cube is 10 cm.

What percentage of the contents of the box is the air that surrounds the cylinder?

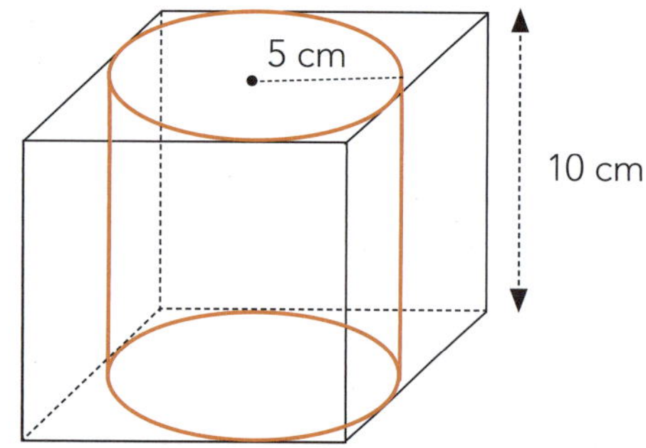

 ISBN: 9780170450454

Challenge 6

The external dimensions of a wooden box are 25 cm by 30 cm by 20 cm. The thickness of the box is 2 cm all around. The bottom is also 2 cm thick.

- Calculate the internal volume of this box.
- Calculate the volume of the wood used to make the box.

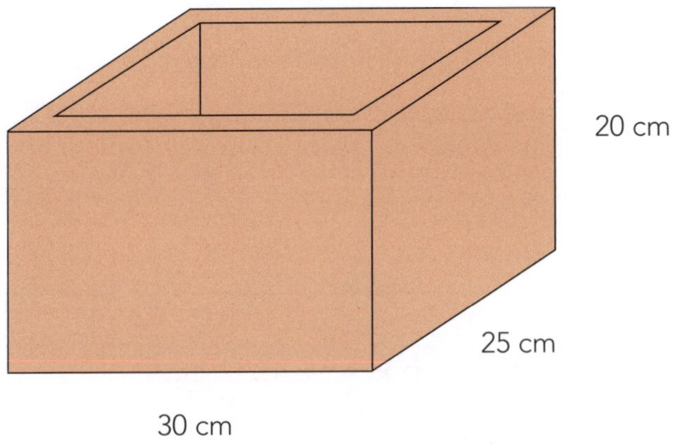

20 cm

25 cm

30 cm

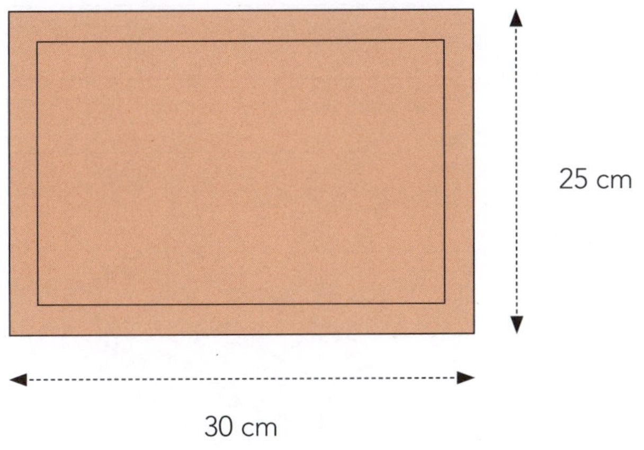

25 cm

30 cm

1 L = 1000 cm^3. Calculate the capacity of the box.

ISBN: 9780170450454

Challenge 7

This shape is made up of eight cubes.
The total volume of the shape is 216 cm^3.

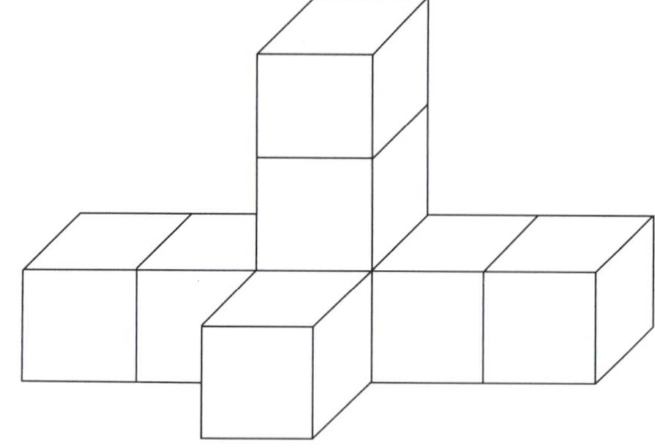

1 What is the volume of one of the cubes?

____

2 What is the length of one side of a cube?

____

3 Calculate the surface area of this shape. Include the 'floor' in your calculations.

Floor = 6 x 9 = ______

Ceiling = ______

Back = ______

Front = ______

Sides = ______

Total = ______

4 Calculate the surface area if the eight blocks are arranged as a cuboid like this.

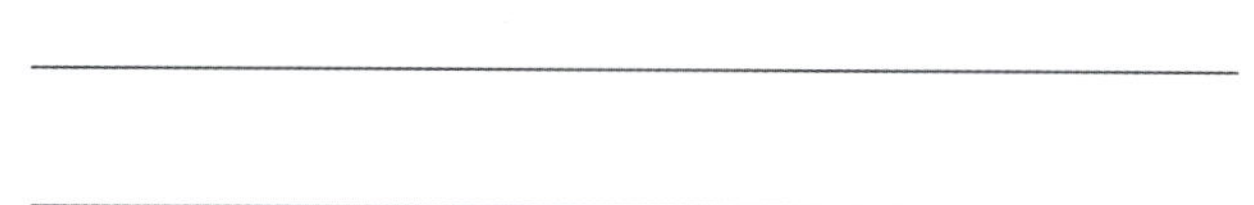

5 Calculate the surface area if the eight blocks are arranged as a cube.

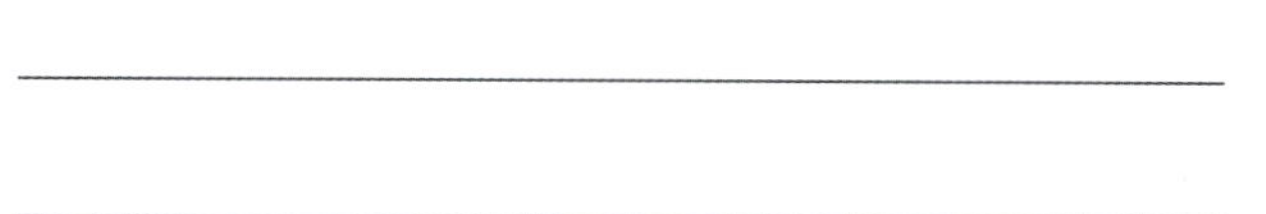

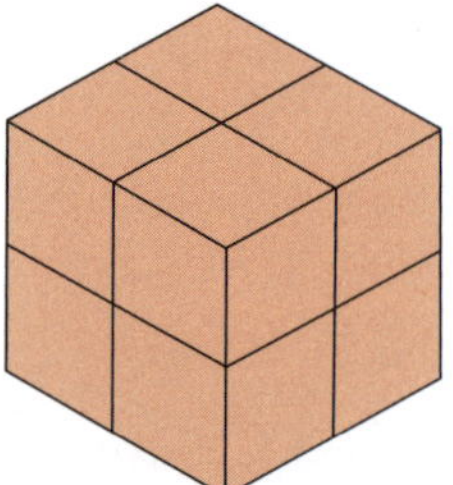

6 The volume of each shape is the same. What do you notice about the surface area as the shapes become more compact?

____

 ISBN: 9780170450454

Challenge 8

Answer the following questions.

1 The volume of a cube is 100 cm^3. Find the length of each side.

2 A jug can hold 100 mL. If the dimensions of a similar jug are double those of the first jug, how much can it hold?

3 Show how this 3 cm by 6 cm piece of card can be cut into two pieces that can be rearranged to form a 2 cm by 9 cm rectangle. You may cut only along the gridlines.

4 On Monday, Grandma's lollipop box contained seven lollipops, and it had a mass of 190 g. On Tuesday, she had refilled the box and it contained 19 lollipops, and it had a mass of 370 g. What is the mass of the empty box?

5 All the shapes in the diagram are squares. The lengths of the sides can only be integers. The small shaded square has an area of 1 cm^2. The large shaded square has an area of 49 cm^2. Calculate the area of the entire diagram.

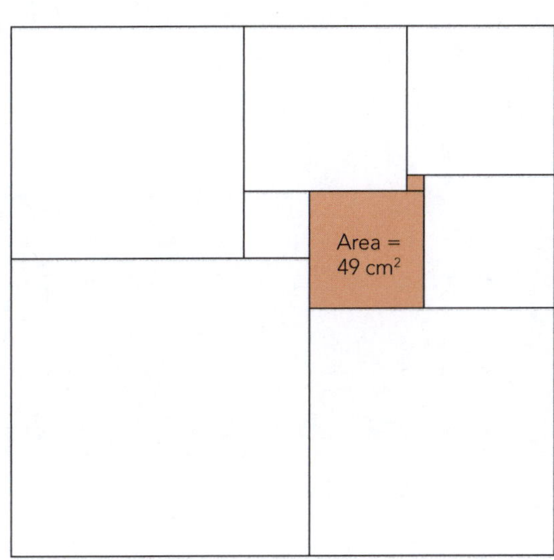

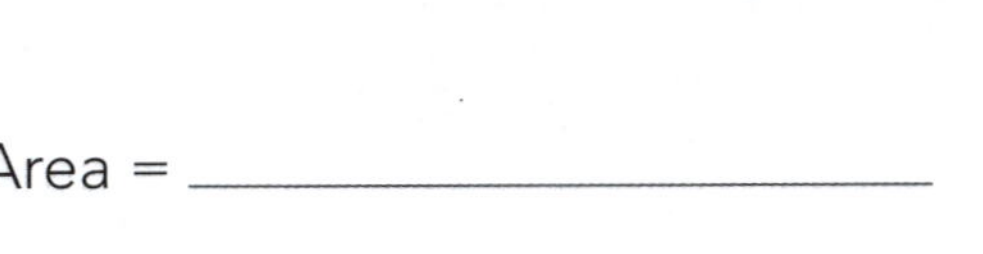

Area = ____________

ISBN: 9780170450454

Challenge 9

Using algebra when solving measurement problems

- Many problems require the use of algebra before they can be solved.
- This usually involves rearranging formulas.
- The rules for this are the same as those used for solving equations.

Rules:
1. You can do anything you like to an expression as long as you do the **same to both sides**.
2. There should be only **one equals sign** per line.
3. Move the variable you want to the left of the equals sign, and everything else to the right.
4. When you want to get rid of something from one side, perform the **opposite operation**.
5. Once you have the variable that you need on its own on the left, **substitute** the values you know.
6. Don't forget to add the **units** to your answer.

Examples:

1 The circumference of a circle needs to be 71 cm. What should its radius be?

$2\pi r = C$ — Put what you want (r) on the left.

$r = \dfrac{C}{2\pi}$ — Get rid of the 2 and the π from the left by dividing.

$= \dfrac{71}{2\pi}$ — Substitute the values you know.

$= 11.3$ cm — Don't forget the units.

2 The volume of a cylinder is 13 949.3 cm^3 and its height is 20 cm. Calculate its radius.

$\pi r^2 h = V$ — Put what you want (r) on the left.

$r^2 = \dfrac{V}{\pi h}$ — Get rid of the π and the h from the left by dividing.

$r = \sqrt{\dfrac{V}{\pi h}}$ — 'Undo' the square by taking the square root.

$= \sqrt{\dfrac{13\,949.3}{\pi \times 20}}$ — Substitute the values you know.

$= 14.9$ cm — Don't forget the units.

 ISBN: 9780170450454

Rearrange the following formulas, and find the required values.

1 The area of a parallelogram is 104.5 cm^2 and its base is 9.5 cm. Calculate its vertical height.

Area = $b \times h$

2 Kerry has to construct a cuboid that has a volume of 663 cm^3. If its height has to be 8.5 cm and its depth must be 10.4 cm, how wide must it be?

Volume = $h \times w \times d$

3 The volume of a cube is 1.728 m^3. Calculate the length of its base.

Volume = b^3

4 The area of a circle is 834.7 cm^2. Calculate its radius.

Area = πr^2

5 A triangular prism has a volume of 818.4 cm^3. The base of the triangle is 12.4 cm and its height is 8 cm. Calculate the length of the prism.

Volume = $\frac{1}{2} \times b \times h \times l$

ISBN: 9780170450454

6 A cylinder with a radius of 1.7 m has a volume of 91.7 m^3. Calculate its height.

Volume = $\pi r^2 h$

7 A cylinder with a height of 4 cm has a volume of 353 cm^3. Calculate its radius.

Volume = $\pi r^2 h$

8 A trapezium has parallel sides of 8.4 cm and 13.2 cm. Its area is 114.48 cm^2. Calculate its height.

$$A = \frac{a + b}{2} \times h$$

9 A trapezium has an area of 363.6 cm^2. Its height is 18 cm and one of its parallel sides is 15.6 cm. Calculate the length of the other parallel side.

$$A = \frac{a + b}{2} \times h$$

 ISBN: 9780170450454

Revision 1

1 Write the abbreviations for these units.

a centimetre ____________ **b** kiljoule ____________

c millilitre ____________ **d** cubic metre ____________

2 Write the meaning of these abbreviations.

a tbsp ____________ **b** °C ____________

c cm^2 ____________ **d** ha ____________

3 Convert these measurements.

a 9 cm = ____________ mm **b** 0.1 t = ____________ kg

c 350 mL = ____________ L **d** 389 cm = ____________ m

e 700 g = ____________ kg **f** 0.4 km = ____________ m

g 25 g = ____________ mg **h** 2.4 L = ____________ mL

4 Circle or highlight the most likely unit of measurement for these items.

a The amount of milk in your cereal.

kg mL cm L

b The length of your sock.

km g t cm

c The mass of a goldfish.

L kg mm g

d The length of a flute.

m km cm kg

5 One paper clip weighs, on average, one gram. How many kilograms (kg) would a packet of 2500 weigh?

____

6 Miriam's new house is 3.4 km from her school. How many metres (m) is this?

____

ISBN: 9780170450454

7 What speed is this car doing?

____

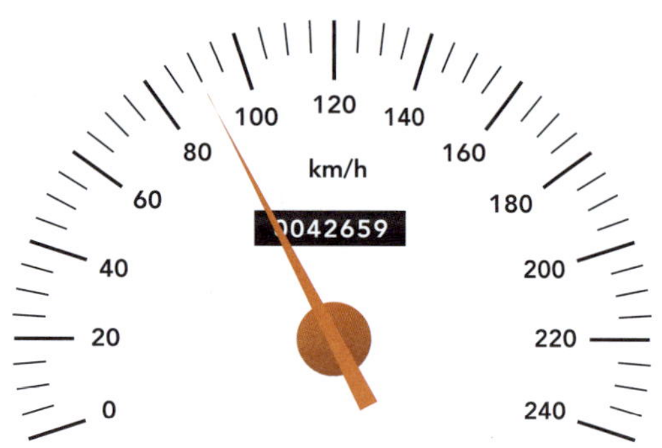

8 Add a line to this protractor to show 132°.

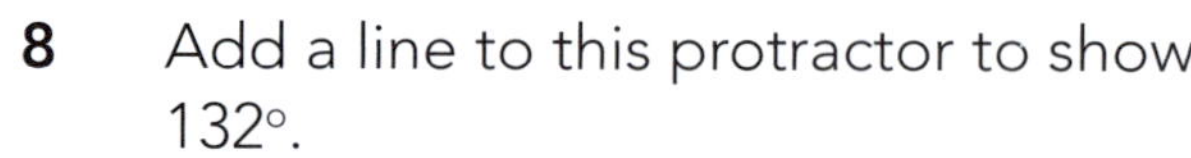

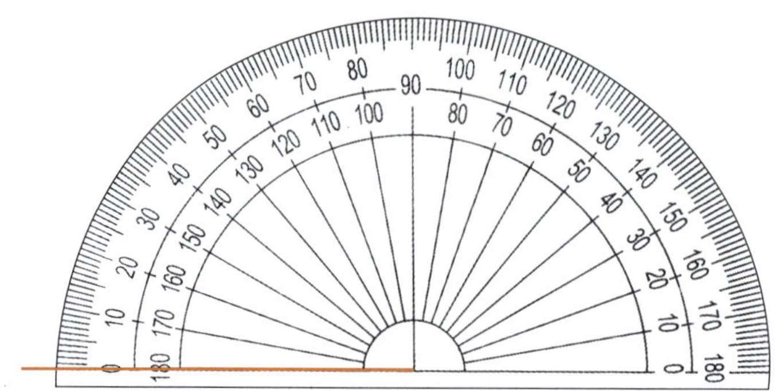

9 Calculate the perimeters of these shapes.

a

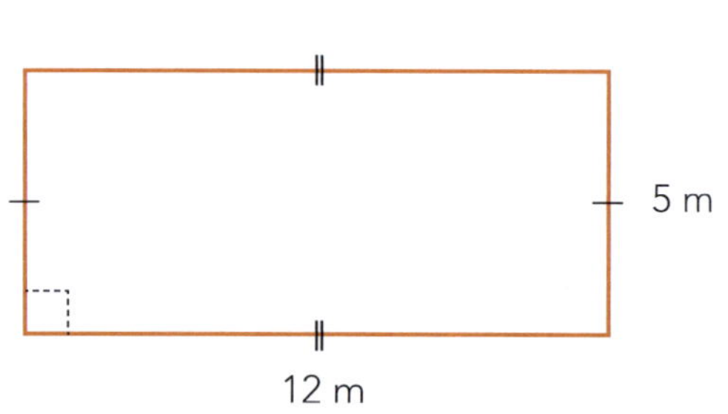

____

____

b

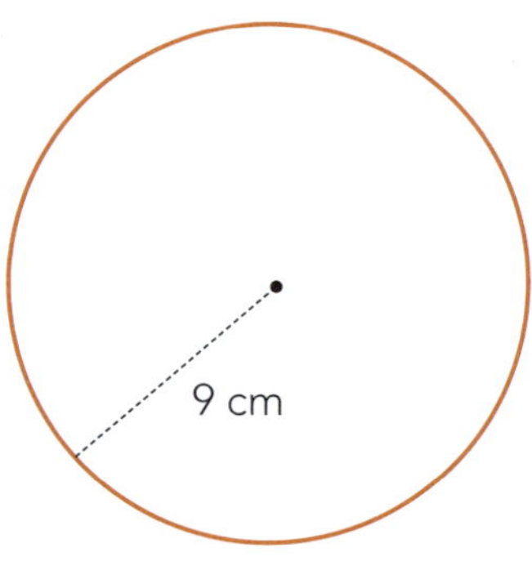

____

____

10 Calculate the areas of these shapes.

a

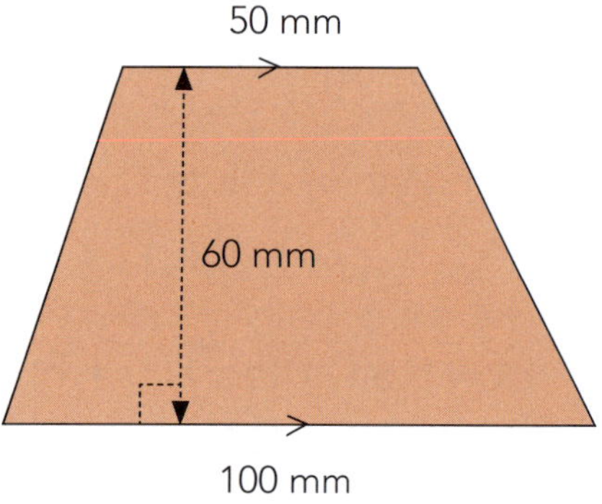

____

____

b

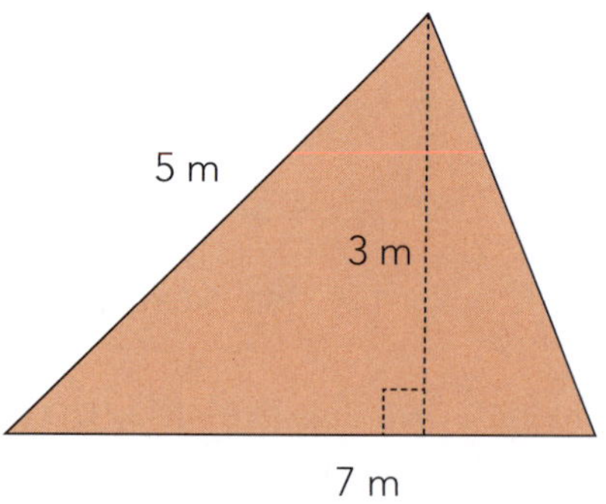

____

____

 ISBN: 9780170450454

c

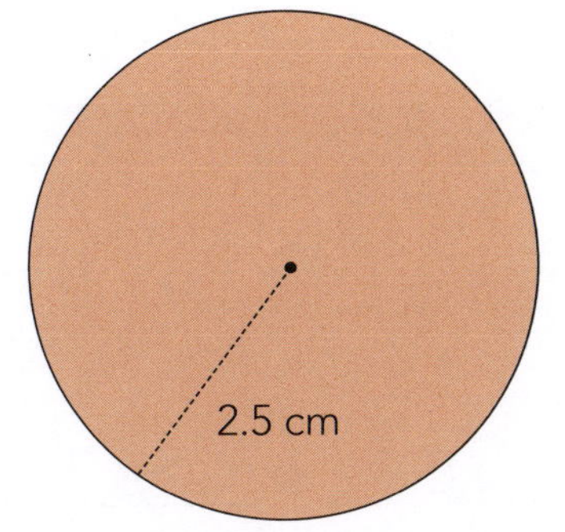

d

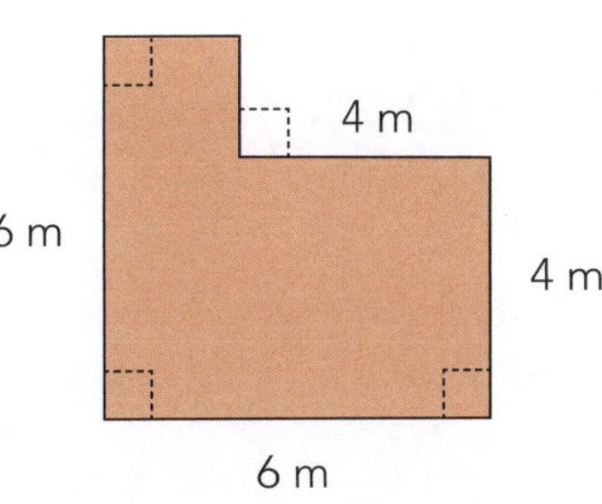

____

____

____

____

11 Calculate the volumes of these shapes.

a

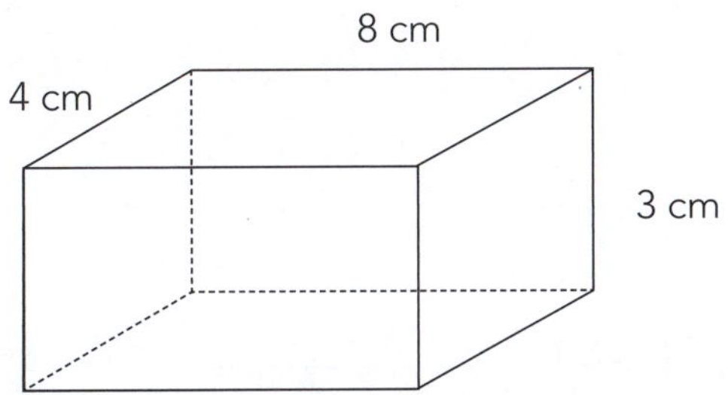

b

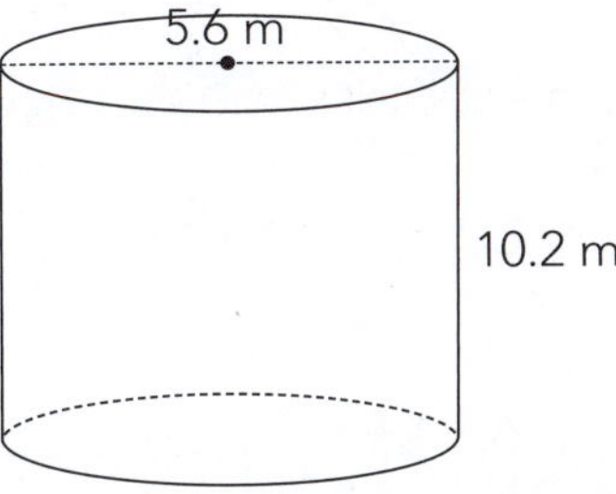

____

____

____

____

c

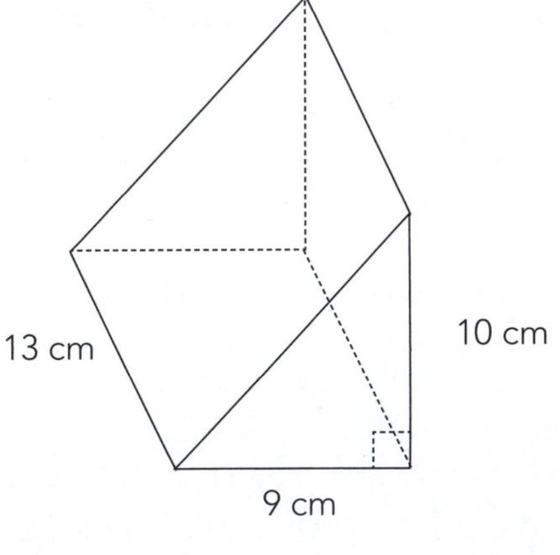

d

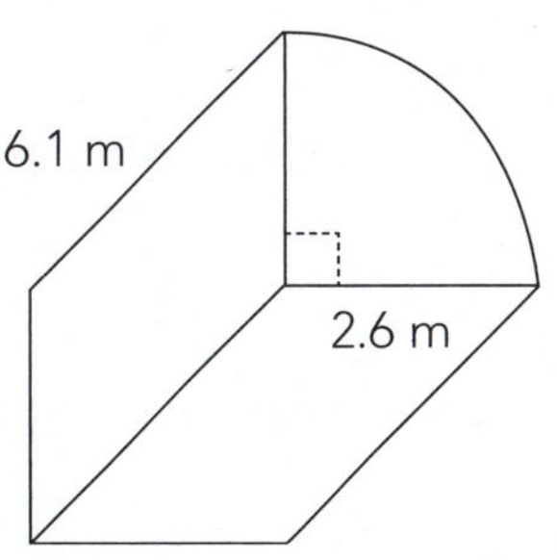

____

____

____

____

ISBN: 9780170450454

Revision 2

1 Write the abbreviations for these units.

a metre ____________ b hectare ____________

c calorie ____________ d cubic kilometre ____________

2 Write the meaning of these abbreviations.

a tsp ____________ b cc ____________

c GB ____________ d m^2 ____________

3 Convert these measurements.

a 80 mm = ____________ cm b 450 g = ____________ kg

c 6.5 L = ____________ mL d 2.75 m = ____________ cm

e 9.1 kg = ____________ g f 6740 cm = ____________ m

g 0.34 km = ____________ m h 350 mL = ____________ L

4 Circle or highlight the most likely unit of measurement for these items.

a The amount of juice in a glass.

km mL g L

b The mass of a sandwich.

L g t kg

c The length of a garage.

km mL m mg

d The mass of a bicycle.

km g cm kg

5 A box contains 8 bags of sugar. If the empty box weighs 450 g, and the full box weighs a total of 12 450 g, what is the mass of each bag of sugar in kilograms (kg)?

____

6 Joshua runs 4300 m a day. How many kilometres (km) would he run in a week?

____

 ISBN: 9780170450454

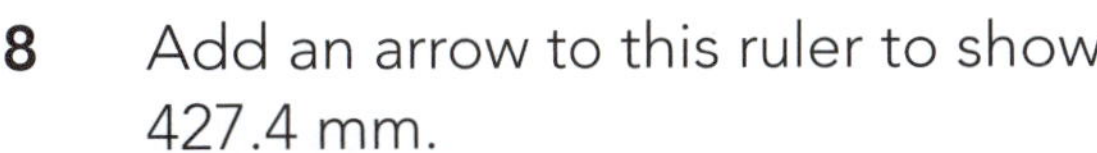

7 Identify the measurement given by this pointer.

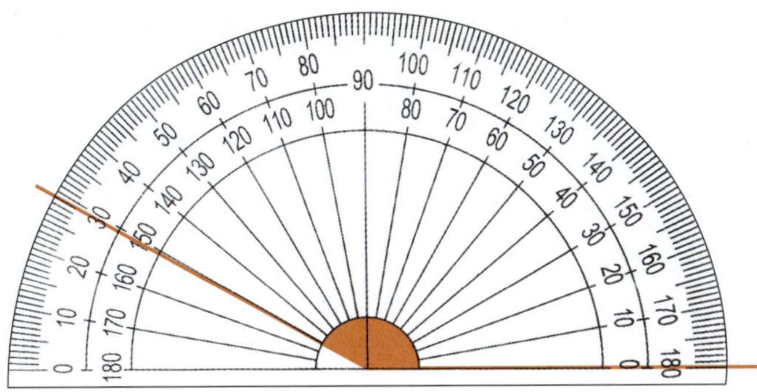

8 Add an arrow to this ruler to show 427.4 mm.

9 Find the perimeters of these shapes.

a

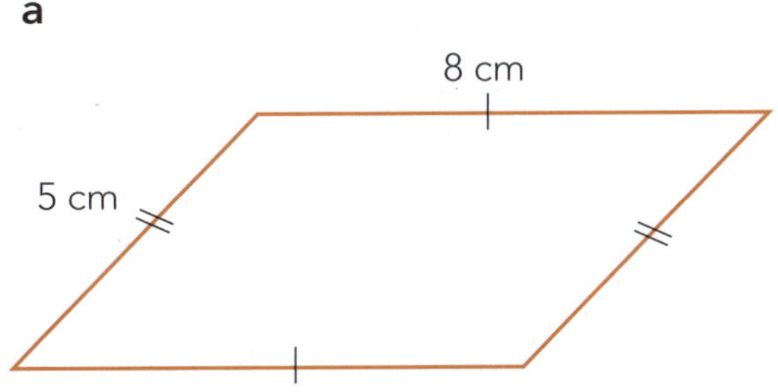

b

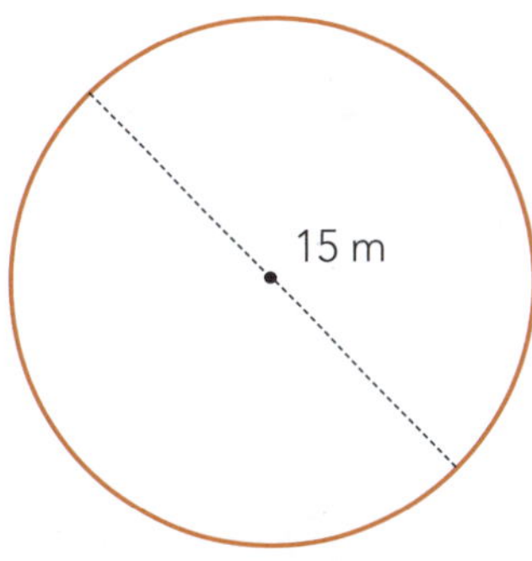

10 Find the shaded areas of these shapes.

a

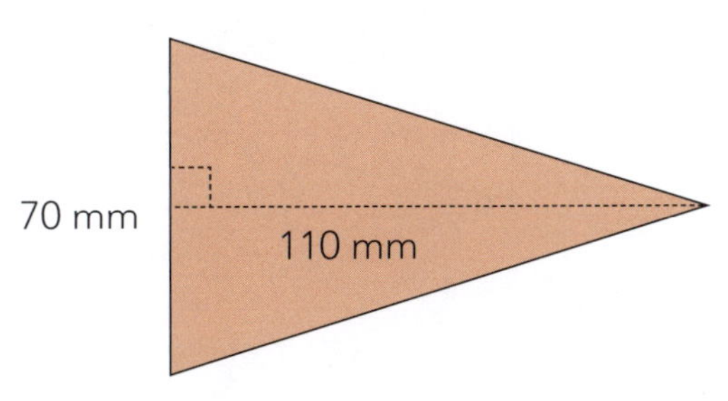

b

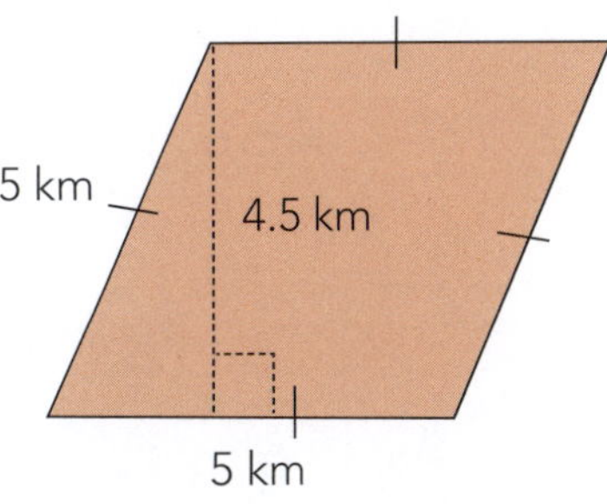

ISBN: 9780170450454

c

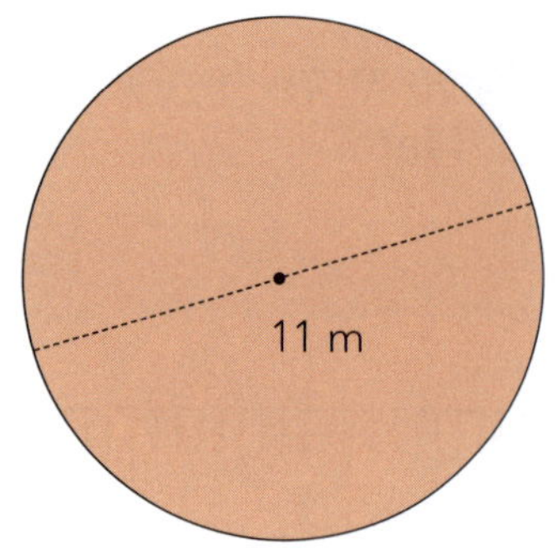

d

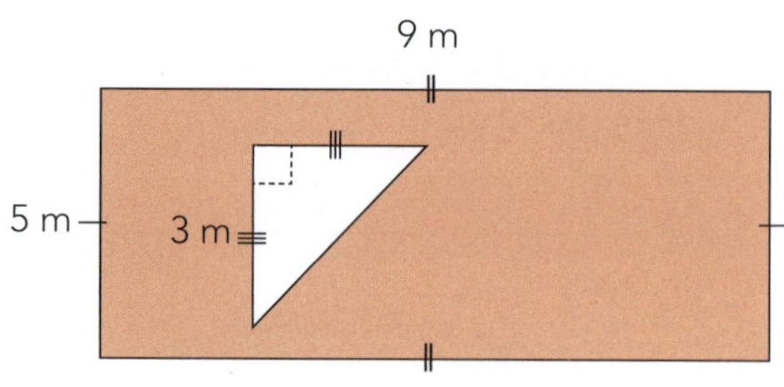

11 Find the volumes of these shapes.

a

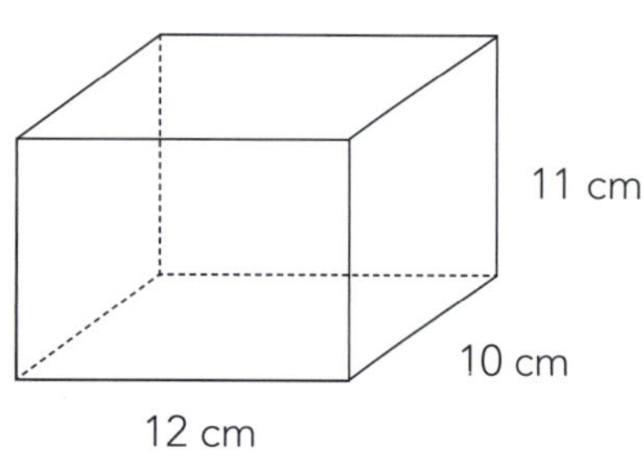

b

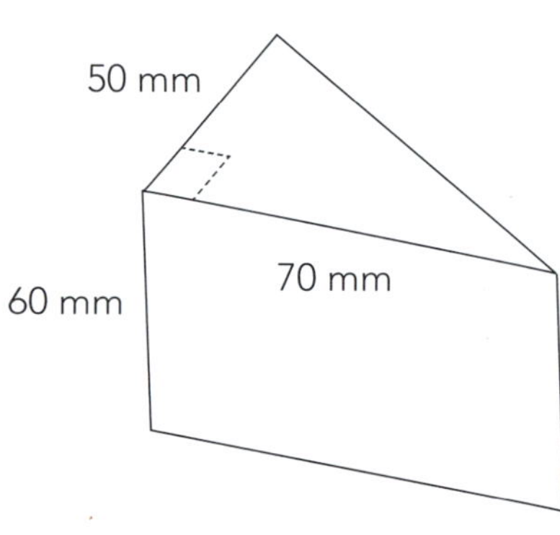

c

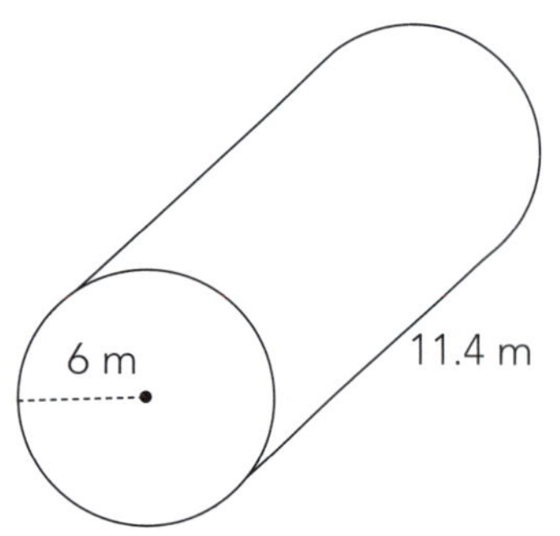

d

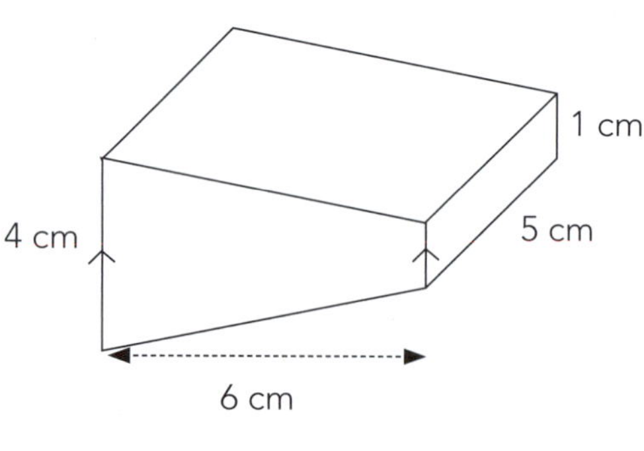

 ISBN: 9780170450454

Answers

The language of measurement (p. 6)

Length: distance, far, stretch, long, wide, reach
Time: era, long, period, age
Volume/Capacity: room, bulk, space
Angle: incline, decline, slant, steep, gradient, pitch, slope, flat
Temperature: warm, cold, heat, hot, fever, icy
Mass: heavy, load, light

Measuring devices (p. 7)

Length: tape measure, ruler, pedometer, odometer
Mass: scales, spring balance
Time: stopwatch, timer, clock
Capacity: cup, syringe, teaspoon, tablespoon, measuring cylinder, pipette, measuring cup
Angle: protractor, compass, clinometer
Temperature: thermometer

Units (pp. 8–20)

Abbreviations (shortened versions) for units (p. 8)

Unit of measurement	Shortened version	Used to measure
Second	s	time
Centimetre	cm	length
Megabyte	MB	data
Kilometre	km	length
Degree Celsius	°C	temperature
Kilogram	kg	mass
Litre	L	capacity
Millilitre	mL	capacity
Millimetre	mm	length
Tablespoon	tbsp	capacity
Calorie	cal	energy
Hectare	ha	area
Tonne	t	mass
Metre	m	length
Minute	min	time
Milligram	mg	mass
Cup	c	capacity
Gigabyte	GB	data
Teaspoon	tsp	capacity
Gram	g	mass
Kilojoule	kJ	energy
Cubic metre	m^3	volume
Square metre	m^2	area
Cubic centimetre	cm^3	volume

Length (pp. 9–11)

1 180 mm
2 25 000 cm
3 360 000 cm
4 0.543 m
5 2010 mm
6 199 900 cm
7 0.7 cm
8 5 km
9 1200 cm
10 4000 m
11 0.19 m
12 75 mm
13 160 000 cm
14 1.2 m
15 1000 mm
16 0.0269 km
17 0.87 km
18 200 000 mm
19 150 mm
20 26 m
21 3320 m
22 658 mm
23 0.04 m
24 9999 mm
25 21 mm, 12 cm, 106 cm, 1.5 m, 0.5 km
26 0.989 km, 989 001 mm, 98 901 cm, 990 m, 998 m
27 m
28 mm
29 cm
30 km
31 m
32 mm
33 cm
34 mm
35 km
36 m
37 cm
38 km
39 15.5 cm
40 40 mm
41 23.77 m
42 2.4 m
43 42.2 km
44 0.81 m
45 84 mm
46 8 mm

Mass (pp. 12–14)

1 1.3 kg
2 2100 kg
3 640 g
4 8.9 g
5 6760 mg
6 32 200 g
7 9900 g
8 0.00887 t
9 16 000 g
10 900 kg
11 0.63 g
12 0.785 kg
13 94 000 mg
14 0.236 t
15 1 400 000 mg
16 0.256 t
17 1 300 000 g
18 0.007632 kg
19 0.000341 t
20 64 000 000 mg
21 82 g
22 43 kg
23 0.11 kg
24 7545 mg
25 9960 g
26 0.0009899 t
27 610 000 mg, 6100 g, 0.060 t, 61 kg, 61 100 g
28 2 012 000 g, 2021 kg, 2.12 t, 2201 kg, 2.21 t

ISBN: 9780170450454

29	kg	**30**	t
31	g	**32**	mg
33	t	**34**	g
35	mg	**36**	g
37	kg	**38**	g
39	kg	**40**	t
41	12 g	**42**	181.4 kg
43	4.7 kg	**44**	250 g
45	5000 t	**46**	700 g
47	0.0082 g	**48**	1 kg

Capacity (pp. 15–16)

1	0.23 L	**2**	650 mL
3	8.9 mL	**4**	9.969 L
5	68 000 mL	**6**	0.463 L
7	6.3 L	**8**	1000 mL
9	2400 mL	**10**	10.5 L
11	0.001 L	**12**	990 mL

13 0.919 L, 0.99 L, 991 mL, 999 mL, 1 L

14 1001 mL, 1.01 L, 1.1 L, 1.101 L, 1110 mL

15	1.5 L	**16**	0.35 mL
17	10 L	**18**	25 L
19	5 mL	**20**	250 L
21	250 mL	**22**	22 mL
23	1000 L		

Conversion cross-number (p. 17)

[1] 7	[2] 5		[3] 3	[4] 1	[5] 2	4		[6] 4
	[7] 8	2	.	6	7		[8] 5	7
[9] 1	2		[10] 9	0	.	[11] 3		2
[12] 9		[13] 3	6		[14] 5	.	[15] 1	
[16] 4	[17] 1	0				[18] 7	0	[19] 9
	[20] 8	.	[21] 6		[22] 1	3		.
[23] 9		[24] 8	.	[25] 7	3		[26] 2	9
[27] 5	7		[28] 4	2	3	.	2	
0		[29] 1	5	1	0		[30] 2	1

Appropriate units (p. 18)

1	g	**2**	mg
3	cm	**4**	mL
5	kg	**6**	g
7	mL	**8**	m
9	cm	**10**	g
11	L	**12**	t
13	kg	**14**	m
15	mg	**16**	g

Estimating quantities (p. 19)

1	5.4 m	**2**	21 196 km
3	1.5 L	**4**	63 g
5	1.2 cm	**6**	324 m
7	160 kg	**8**	30.5 m
9	760 mm	**10**	400 mL
11	9.5 t	**12**	5.2 km
13	62 mm	**14**	200 g
15	1 250 000 L	**16**	2500 L
17	8 L	**18**	290 cm
19	3 kg	**20**	8 mg

Word questions (p. 20)

1	250 mL	**2**	Mason ran 90 m further
3	1.596 L	**4**	1.89 t
5	3.4 so 3 presents	**6**	75 g
7	**a** 52	**b**	Yes; only 50
8	1.14 g	**9**	0.104 mm

Scales (pp. 21–24)

Reading scales (pp. 21–22)

1 A = 0.3 cm
B = 3.8 cm
C = 6.1 cm

2 D = 16°
E = 124°

3 –7.5°C

4 250 V

5 450 mL

6 F = 100.4 mm
G = 101.6 mm
H = 102.8 mm

7 2700 r/min

8 I = 225°

Showing values on scales (pp. 23–24)

1

2

3

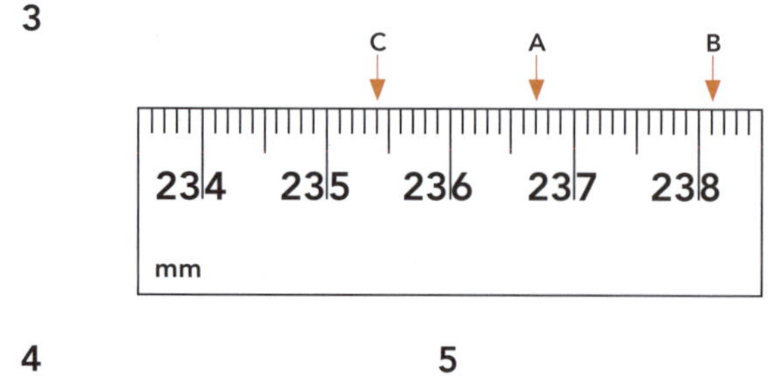

4

5

 ISBN: 9780170450454

6 7

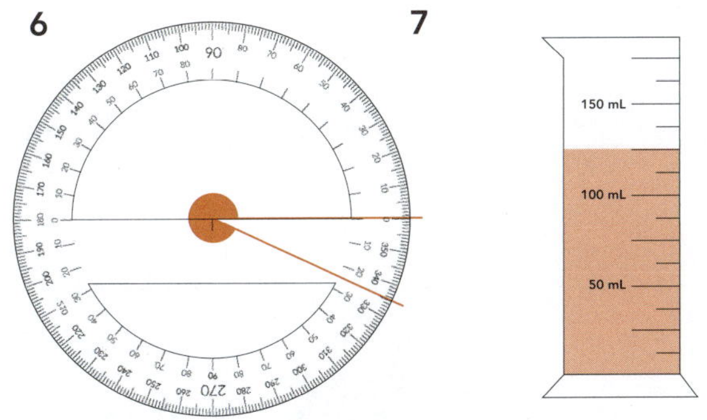

8

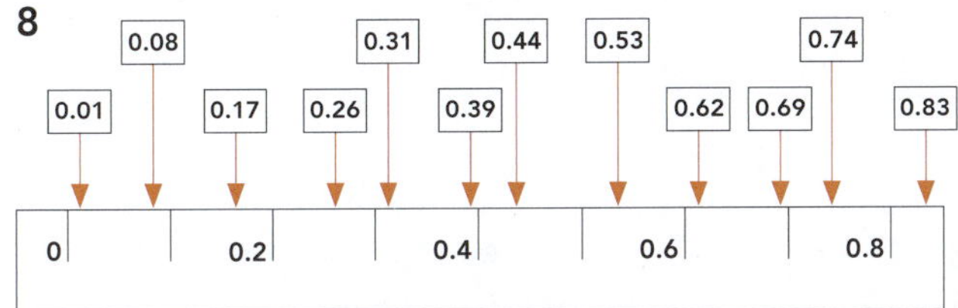

Perimeter (pp. 25–37)

Shapes with linear sides (pp. 25–28)

1	22 cm	2	12 mm
3	14 m	4	12 cm
5	24 cm	6	20 cm
7	11 m	8	15 km
9	12 m	10	10 cm
11	14 mm	12	31.5 cm
13	18 cm or 180 mm	14	146 cm
15	5.4 km or 5400 m	16	18 km or 18 000 m
17	19.5 m	18	13 cm
19	6 m	20	12 cm
21	32 km	22	16 cm
23	950 m	24	54 m
25	3 m	26	0.82 m
27	6 m by 4 m	28	320 m

Circles (pp. 29–31)

1	25.13 m	2	12.57 km
3	37.70 cm	4	213.63 mm
5	31.42 m	6	0.94 km
7	28.27 cm	8	38.64 cm
9	34.56 m	10	18.84 km
11	25.71 cm	12	12.85 km
13	11.05 m	14	437.04 mm
15	10.71 cm	16	6.71 m

Compound shapes (pp. 32–33)

1	34 m	2	30 cm
3	40 km	4	50 cm
5	10 m	6	31 km
7	565.62 mm	8	215.54 cm
9	16.37 m	10	281 cm

Word questions (pp. 34–35)

1	a	45.3 m	b	60.4 m
2	a	13.51 m	b	193
3	a	240 cm	b	188.5 cm
4	a	60 cm	b	19 cm
5	a	8.1 m	b	10

Challenge 1 (p. 36)

73.47 cm

Challenge 2 (p. 37)

1	4 cm	2	35 m
3	None (the ship floats)	4	208 mm
5	192 cm	6	1.55 m

Area (pp. 38–64)

Units of area (p. 38)

1	0.6 ha	2	0.07 km^2
3	0.095 m^2	4	0.81 m^2
5	4.5 km^2	6	98 ha
7	10.1 m^2	8	1 030 000 m^2

Quadrilaterals (pp. 39–44)

Square and rectangle (pp. 39–40)

1	24 cm^2	2	9 mm^2
3	16 km^2	4	22 cm^2
5	12 cm^2	6	4 m^2
7	64 mm^2	8	72 m^2
9	6 km	10	7 cm
11	Check with your teacher if you have a different answer.	12	A square with 9 cm sides.

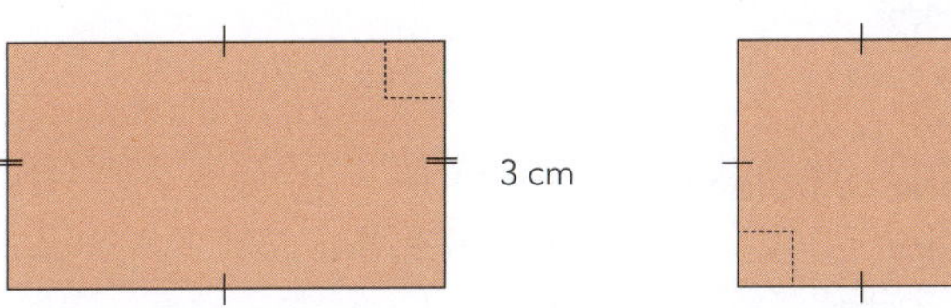

Parallelogram and rhombus (pp. 41–42)

1	42 km^2	2	36 mm^2
3	14 cm^2	4	80 m^2
5	12 km^2	6	0.06 m^2
7	30 m^2	8	55 cm^2
9	7 cm	10	9 m
11	Check with your teacher if you have a different answer.	12	Check with your teacher if you have a different answer.

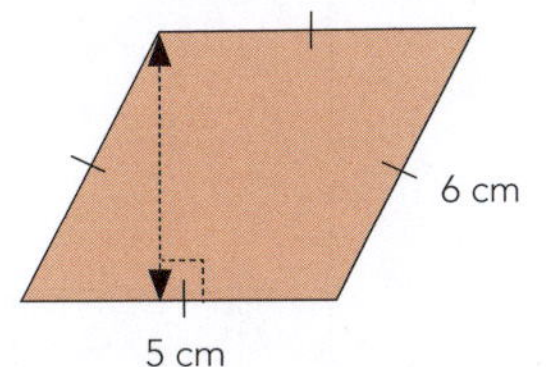

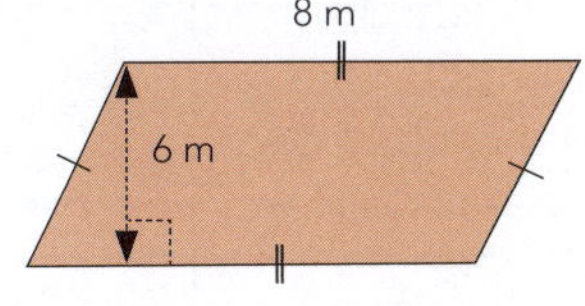

Trapezium (pp. 43–44)

1	45 km^2	2	39 mm^2
3	19.5 m^2	4	66 cm^2
5	9 km^2	6	132 mm^2
7	7 m	8	7 km

ISBN: 9780170450454

Triangles (pp. 45–46)

1 8 km^2 **2** 300 mm^2
3 15 cm^2 **4** 27 m^2
5 8 mm^2 **6** 15 m^2
7 8 mm **8** 12 cm
9 Check with your teacher if you have a different answer.
10 Check with your teacher if you have a different answer.

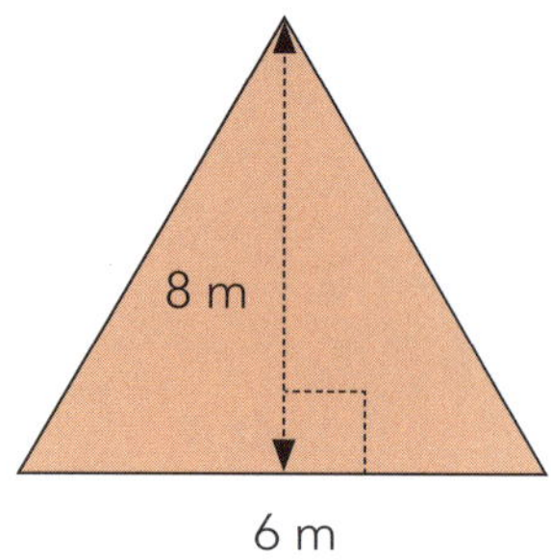

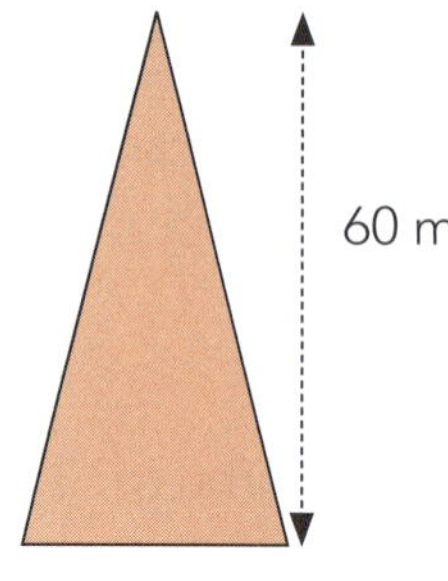

Circles (pp. 47–49)

1 314.16 cm^2 **2** 380.13 mm^2
3 254.47 m^2 **4** 176.71 cm^2
5 3.46 km^2 **6** 80 424.77 mm^2
7 5.31 m^2 **8** 2206.18 mm^2
9 14.14 m^2 **10** 265.46 mm^2
11 7.07 cm^2 **12** 58.90 m^2
13 15 km **14** 46 m
15 5.80 cm **16** 327 mm (0 dp)

Compound shapes (pp. 50–51)

1 26 mm^2 **2** 30 km^2
3 66 m^2 **4** 45 cm^2
5 30 m^2 **6** 42 mm^2
7 102.52 cm^2 **8** 25 m^2
9 83.22 m^2 **10** 0.76 km^2

Shapes with holes (pp. 52–53)

1 41 km^2 **2** 45.5 mm^2
3 67.73 cm^2 **4** 173.56 m^2
5 40 cm^2 **6** 2.56 km^2
7 98.17 m^2 **8** 67.875 cm^2
9 5087.5 mm^2 **10** 90.24 km^2

Summary (p. 70)

Complete the table:

Shape	Picture	Formula
Quadrilateral (square, rectangle, rhombus and parallelogram)	height, base	$A = b \times h$
Trapezium	a, height, b	$A = \frac{a+b}{2} \times h$

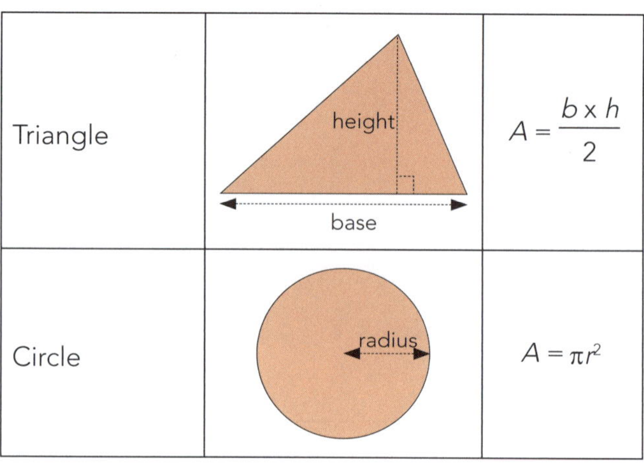

Triangle	height, base	$A = \frac{b \times h}{2}$
Circle	radius	$A = \pi r^2$

Mixing it up (pp. 55–56)

1 50 m^2 **2** 44 cm^2
3 21 km^2 **4** 153.94 mm^2
5 72 mm^2 **6** 364 cm^2
7 61.75 cm^2 **8** 0.24 m^2
9 0.08 km^2 **10** 3042.5 mm^2
11 35.87 cm^2 **12** 118.25 cm^2

Word questions (pp. 57–58)

1 2050.81 m^2 **2** 8781 cm^2 (0 dp)
3 1444 cm^2 **4** 1134.11 cm^2 (2 dp)
5 187.2 cm^2 **6** 45 625 cm^2 (2 dp)
7 **a** 645.88 m^2
b 2 bags with 6.31 kg left over (2 dp)
8 **a** 25.46 m^2
b Needs 4.63 L so 5 L with 0.37 L left over
9 **a** 326.73 cm^2 **b** 898.50 cm^2

Challenge 3 (p. 59)

1 **a** 21.46% **b** 21.46%
c They are the same.
d 42.92% **e** 42.92%
f They are the same.
g 42.81% **h** 14.27%

Challenge 4 (p. 60)

1 56 m^2 **2** 12 m
3

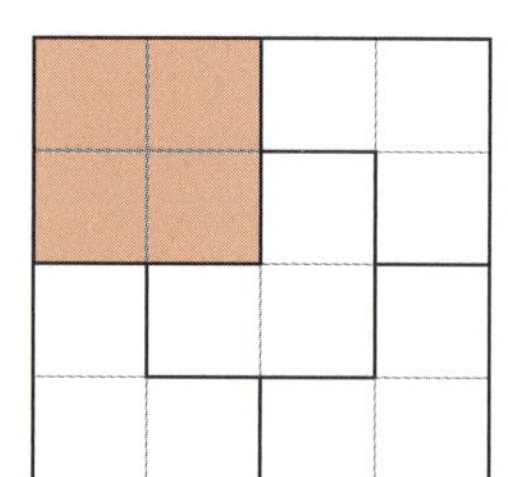

4 The square one because its area is 324 cm^2, whereas the round one is 314 cm^2.
5 35 m^2

Surface area (pp. 61–62)

1 2400 cm^2 **2** 5200 cm^2
3 1256.64 cm^2 **4** 15 079.64 cm^2

ISBN: 9780170450454

5 8 cm
6 3 cm, 5 cm, 7 cm
7 450 cm^2

Challenge 5 (pp. 63–64)

1 Area = 15 x **12**
= 180 cm^2
What went wrong: Used slant height of the parallelogram (13 cm) rather than vertical height (12 cm).

2 Area = **2 x π x 7**
= 43.98 **cm** (2 dp)
What went wrong: Used the formula for area (πr^2) rather than that for circumference ($2\pi r$) and used units for area (cm^2) rather than length (cm).

3 Area = $\frac{1}{2}$ x **29** x **140**
= 2030 mm^2
What went wrong: Triangle base is 29 mm, not 171 mm, and 14 cm not converted to 140 mm.

4 Area = $\frac{1}{2}$ x π x **9**^{2}
= 127.23 cm^2
What went wrong: Used the diameter (18 cm) rather than the radius (9 cm) in calculation.

5 Area of one face = $\frac{8.64}{6}$
= 1.44 m^2
So edge length = **1.44**
= 1.2 m
What went wrong: Length of an edge is the square root of the area, not one quarter of it.

6 Perimeter = (**4** x 4) + ($\frac{1}{2}$ x π x 8)
= 28.57 cm (2 dp)
What went wrong: Left out the radius of the circle.

7 SA = (**2** x π x 0.75^2) + (2π x 0.75 x 2.1)
= 13.43 m^2 (2 dp)
What went wrong: Didn't include both the top and the bottom of the cylinders.

8 SA = 5[(2 x 0.12 x 4) + (2 x **0.05** x 4) + (2 x **0.05** x 0.12)]
= 5[1.372]
= 6.86 m^2
What went wrong: Incorrect conversion of units: 5 cm = 0.05 m, not 0.5 m.

Volume (pp. 65–84)

Units of volume (p. 65)

1 0.005 m^3
2 0.009 m^3
3 0.0006 m^3
4 7 200 000 cm^3
5 1100 cm^3
6 99 000 cm^3

Prisms (p. 66)

1  ✗
2 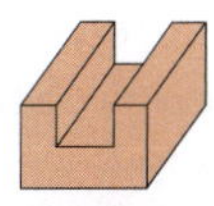 ✓
3 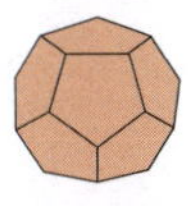 ✗
4 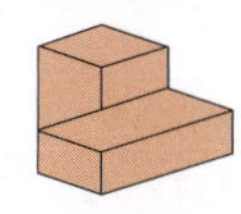 ✗
5 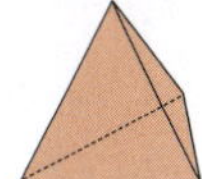 ✗
6 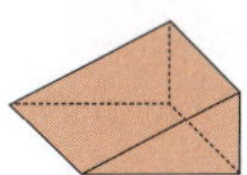 ✓

Cuboids (pp. 67–68)

1 336 mm^3
2 64 cm^3
3 55 m^3
4 65.625 cm^3
5 118 125 cm^3
6 0.023115 m^3
7 4 m, 2 m, 1 m
8 12 cm
9 5000

Compound cuboids (pp. 69–70)

1 21 460 mm^3
2 4320 cm^3
3 0.021 km^3
4 36 252 cm^3
5 0.465 m^3
6 29 832 mm^3
7 11 515 cm^3
8 3392.59 cm^3
9 1.52 m^3
10 16 456 cm^3

Triangular prisms (pp. 71–72)

1 12 m^3
2 455 625 mm^3
3 292.5 cm^3
4 0.04 m^3
5 173 664 cm^3
6 11 339 000 cm^3
7 672 m^3
8 15 cm^3

Other prisms (pp. 73–74)

1 14.35 m^3
2 21 200 mm^3
3 594 cm^3
4 240 030 cm^3
5 275 096 250 mm^3
6 4.16 m^3
7 15 276 cm^3
8 15 m^3

Cylinders (pp. 75–76)

1 31.81 m^3
2 184 763 cm^3
3 2 237 116 mm^3
4 1 082 605.40 cm^3
5 46.80 m^3
6 4624.42 cm^3
7 4 383 405.33 cm^3
8 0.82 cm^3

Word questions (pp. 77–78)

1 3375 cm^3
2 0.69 m^3
3 810 000 mm^3
4 3 cm, 5 cm, 11 cm
5 Height 12 cm, width 6 cm
6 3118.5 mm^3, 3.1185 cm^3
7 444.4 so 445 bottles
8 Total volume = 603.19 cm^3
Internal volume = 503.20 cm^3
Glass = 99.99 cm^3
9 a 7 glasses
b No. Volume = 7.85 glasses, so you still cannot fill an eighth glass.

ISBN: 9780170450454

10 Volumes are 645.22 cm^3, 648.74 cm^3 and 650.23 cm^3, respectively, so she should select the cylinder because its volume is closest to 650 cm^3 and because it is the only shape to hold more than 650 cm^3.

11 21.46%

Challenge 6 (p. 79)

Internal volume = 9828 cm^3
Volume of wood = 5172 cm^3
Capacity = 9.828 L

Challenge 7 (p. 80)

1 27 cm^3 **2** 3 cm

3 Floor = 6 x 9 = 54 cm^2
Ceiling = 6 x 9 = 54 cm^2
Back = 7 x 9 = 63 cm^2
Front = 7 x 9 = 63 cm^2
Side = 8 x 9 = 72 cm^2
Total = 34 x 9 = 306 cm^2

4 28 x 9 = 252 cm^2

5 4 x 6 x 9 = 216 cm^2

6 The surface area becomes smaller.

Challenge 8 (p. 81)

1 4.64 cm **2** 800 mL

3

4 85 g **5** 1056 cm^2

Challenge 9 (pp. 82–84)

1 $h = \frac{A}{b}$
$= 11$ cm

2 $w = \frac{V}{hd}$
$= 7.5$ cm

3 $b = \sqrt[3]{V}$
$= 1.2$ m

4 $r = \sqrt{\frac{A}{\pi}}$
$= 16.3$ cm

5 $l = \frac{2V}{b \times h}$
$= 16.5$ cm

6 $h = \frac{V}{\pi r^2}$
$= 10.1$ m

7 $r = \sqrt{\frac{V}{\pi \times h}}$
$= 5.3$ cm

8 $h = \frac{2A}{a + b}$
$= 10.6$ cm

9 $b = \frac{2A}{h} - a$
$= 24.8$ cm

Revision 1 (pp. 85–87)

1 **a** cm **b** kJ
c mL **d** m^3

2 **a** tablespoon **b** Degree Celsius
c square centimetre
d hectare

3 **a** 90 mm **b** 100 kg
c 0.35 L **d** 3.89 m
e 0.7 kg **f** 400 m
g 0.025 mg **h** 2400 mL

4 **a** mL **b** cm
c g **d** cm

5 2.5 kg **6** 3400 m

7 90 km/h

8

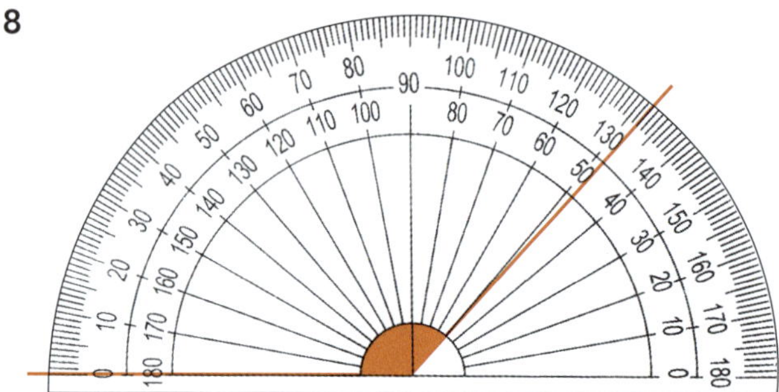

9 **a** 34 m **b** 56.55 cm

10 **a** 4500 mm^2 **b** 10.5 m^2
c 19.63 cm^2 **d** 28 m^2

11 **a** 96 cm^3 **b** 251.23 m^3
c 585 cm^3 **d** 32.39 m^3

Revision 2 (pp. 88–90)

1 **a** m **b** ha
c cal **d** km^3

2 **a** teaspoon **b** cubic centimetre
c gigabyte **d** square metre

3 **a** 8 cm **b** 0.450 kg
c 6500 mL **d** 275 cm
e 9100 g **f** 67.4 m
g 340 m **h** 0.35 L

4 **a** mL **b** g
c m **d** kg

5 1.5 kg **6** 30.1 km

7 151°

8

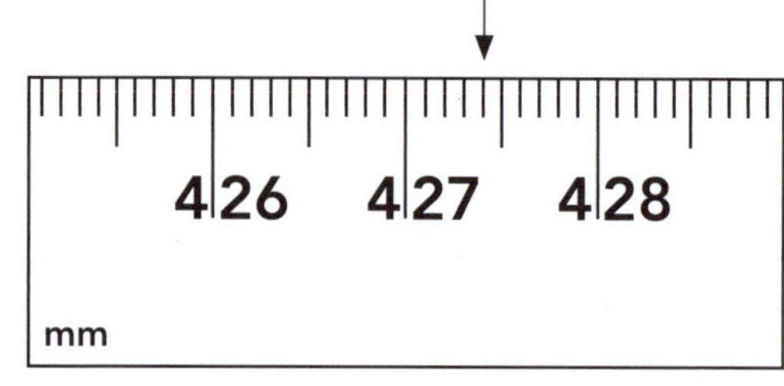

9 **a** 26 cm **b** 47.12 m

10 **a** 3850 mm^2 **b** 22.5 km^2
c 95.03 m^2 **d** 40.5 m^2

11 **a** 1320 cm^3 **b** 105 000 mm^3
c 1289.31 m^3 **d** 75 cm^3

ISBN: 9780170450454